IT ALL BEGINS WITH A HOME

Transformations through Housing

It All Begins With a Home
Transformations through Housing

Copyright © 2014 Single Room Occupancy (SRO) Housing Corporation. All rights reserved.

Single Room Occupancy (SRO) Housing Corporation is recognized as a leader in affordable housing in Los Angeles. The organization serves the Los Angeles Central City East area commonly known as "Skid Row" with a full continuum of housing: Emergency, Transitional, and Permanent Supportive Housing in private rooms and contemporary studio apartments.

SRO Housing Corporation provides clean, safe and affordable housing for over 2,300 homeless and low-income individuals along with a wide array of supportive services for all residents. These include food services, case management, money management, employment services, information and referrals, transportation, community events and outings, socialization and recreation activities. SRO Housing Corporation's diverse and multi-cultural staff includes formerly homeless individuals, residents, and community members.

SRO Housing Corporation
1055 W. 7th St., Suite 3250
Los Angeles, CA 90017
TEL (213) 229-9640
FAX (213) 229-9633
www.srohousing.org
ISBN-13: 978-1497536012
ISBN-10: 1497536014
Library of Congress Control Number: 2014907838
CreateSpace Independent Publishing Platform
North Charleston, South Carolina

IT ALL BEGINS WITH A HOME

Transformations through Housing

*Dedicated to our staff and residents
whose life experiences and insight continue to inspire us.*

FOREWORD

Success Stories

When I first came to the downtown Los Angeles neighborhood known as "Skid Row," I was prepared to encounter homelessness, poverty and despair. I was prepared for the worst and I saw it. Filth, crime and chaos seemed to be everywhere.

And yet, there is great possibility here. I am impressed with the strength of this community and the people in it. I am humbled by the many remarkable journeys that bring people to our doors. I am moved by the courage it takes to rebuild lives that have crumbled. I am inspired by the remarkable resilience of our residents and staff. I am honored to be a part of the transformative process that begins with providing someone with a home. It all begins with a home.

I am grateful to the many individuals who make up SRO Housing Corporation: staff, residents and partners, who contribute to creating the success we celebrate in these stories. These are deeply personal stories, moments of hardship and heartache that shine with dignity and hope. I believe you will enjoy these stories as much as I have.

It is my hope that these stories will inspire you to support our work. From the moment a man or woman comes to SRO Housing and receives a key to their home in Emergency, Transitional or Permanent Supportive Housing, we become their family.

We provide more than a home. We provide supportive services and a sense of belonging and community to our residents. We are proud to **Open Doors and Transform Lives...**

Anita U. Nelson, M.B.A.
Chief Executive Officer
SRO Housing Corporation

CONTENTS

VIRGINIA REED Not just a Survivor, "I am a Conqueror" . . . 3
ROGER ANDERSON From Hobo to HOME 9
KYOUNG WON The Art of Survival 13
SANDRA VALENTINE Carry My Life on My Back 15
DARIUS COFFEY Feeding the Dream 17
CHRIS A Place Where People Love You. 19
DARRIN BROWN My Life Matters to Me Today 25
ROBERT BROWN Connection is Central. 29
MELVIN CRUTCHFIELD Opened the Door 33
WESLEY JONES Sidewalk Sleeping to Local 409. 37
ALAN GARDENER Growing a New Life. 39
HENRY WALLACE Money in the Bank. 43
GEORGE LOFTIN A Person Can Change 47
LAMONT REYNOLDS The Devil Steps In 51
MARK DEAN SOUKUP A Lot More of Everything 53
JEFFREY OWENS Others Can Too 57
JIM THOMPSON Walking the Distance 61
THOMAS JOHNSON I'm Still Alive 67
ETHEL KORMAN Fine, Just Fine. 71

LIBRADA PORTER Principal of Enjoying Life 75
MCKINLEY THOMAS Put a Nickel Aside 79
HORACE HIGGINS Writing with Heart 83
DARNELL GUY Possible to Raise My Kids 87
    A History of Transformation 91
GILBERT CORTEZ Thankful I Got Caught 99
CHARLES BIVIANS A Path From Nothingness 103
DEBORAH MARTIN Creating Something Beautiful 107
DANIEL CASTILLEJA Helping Others Heal 113
EDUARDO "Eddie" PEREZ I Reached My Goal 117
RON SMITH Focused on Helping 119
JONATHAN DAVIS Tragedy into Action 125
OCTAVIA HAMLETT No Longer a Professional Victim . . . 129
MELINDA BOLTON Tired of Living Out of Bags 133
BRENDA WITTEN With a Roof Over My Head 135
ANTHONY VILLARREAL My Own Paris 137
PATRICIA LIPKINS The Happiest Person 141
DENISE DRINKARD PHILLIPS Going to be Awesome 145
LEYMOINE BOLTON Look a Certain Way 149
DEIDRE MAYES It's Temporary 153
TG Hungry for Better Life 157
DAVID The Best Thing That Ever Happened 161
WILLIAM CARR I Never Thought I Would be This Old . . . 165
CHRIS ZAMOR Homeless and Got a Masters Degree 169
DAVID ABEYTA A Father for an Hour 173
A BRIEF HISTORY OF SRO Housing Corporation 177
ABOUT THE ORGANIZATION How You Can Help 179
ABOUT THE BOOK Anita Nelson 181
ABOUT THE AUTHOR Julia Robinson Shimizu 183
ABOUT THE PHOTOGRAPHER
    Rachel Murray Framingheddu 185

INTRODUCTION

SRO Housing Corporation provides housing and supportive services to over 2,300 men and women in downtown Los Angeles. Our residents include veterans, seniors, people who have been chronically homeless and who often live with disabilities including mental illness, physical disabilities and HIV/AIDS. Since we were founded in 1984, we have opened our doors to over 30,000 individuals, transforming lives and our community.

We continue to gather the stories of our residents and staff to illustrate the diversity and dignity of the people we serve. To read more of these stories, visit our website at www.srohousing.org.

**There are many paths to our doors,
these are just a few of them...**

ABUSE

"Every day I have the chance to change someone's life."

Chris

VIRGINIA REED

Not just a survivor, "I am a Conqueror"

> "When I thought of myself as a survivor,
> it also meant I was a victim ... of drugs, alcohol,
> domestic violence, homelessness, cancer.
> But I am no longer a victim, and I am no longer ashamed.
> I am not a survivor. I am a conqueror."

Virginia Reed, affectionately known as 'Ginger' by her fellow SRO Housing co-workers, is the Program Manager for SRO Housing Corporation's Permanent Supportive Housing Programs. Her hard-won wisdom and personal insight serve the community where she lives and works.

It has not been easy. Virginia has conquered decades of debilitating panic disorder, bouts of severe depression, two abusive

IT ALL BEGINS WITH A HOME

and life-threatening marriages, addiction to alcohol and drugs, and the shame and loneliness of living on the streets. She worked to conquer additional challenges to receive a series of degrees with highest academic honors. She graduated Summa Cum Laude with her Associate of Arts Degree in Human Services from Los Angeles Community College (LACC) and was the Valedictorian of her class. She received numerous awards for presentations on regional and national Debate Teams and in Impromptu Speaking and Policy Debate competitions. In 2004, she graduated Summa Cum Laude from California State University, Los Angeles (CSULA) with a Bachelor of Arts degree in Social Work. Later, she was awarded CSULA Alumni Certificate of Honor. She then went on to earn her Master's Degree in Social Work, also Summa Cum Laude. She did all of this while living at SRO Housing Corporation on Skid Row.

Virginia could have walked away with her education, her awards and an impressive catalogue of accolades. But she had a different plan. "When you are a victim of domestic violence, you have to plan your escape. You have to prepare for it and diligently follow it." Instead of escaping Skid Row, Ginger put her life experience to work and decided to stay.

VIRGINIA REED Before and After

"I put down roots here," says Virginia.

VIRGINIA REED

"My goal was always to come back here with the specialized skills that the people we serve need and deserve."

Virginia was raised by her father in a cooperative farming community in Colorado that fostered a sense of belonging. She left her small town and went to live with her mother in the city as a teenager and at 16 had her first child. At 17, she suffered what her doctor called "nerve problems." The symptoms persisted for more than two decades and disrupted every aspect Virginia's life. She experienced extreme physical distress; her head would pound, her heart would race. She feared she was losing control and was afraid she was losing her mind, "I started drinking to control my anxiety. I took the edge off by drinking."

After divorcing her abusive first husband, Virginia followed a long-distance love to California where she was finally diagnosed with a panic disorder. The drugs that controlled her symptoms sent her into a depression that made it impossible to work. Virginia married her long-distance love only to find out he was a 'Dr. Jekyll/Mr. Hyde.' "I was already drinking alcohol and taking excessive amounts of medication. When I started getting beaten, I fled to the streets because I had no place else to go. I was afraid he would find my family and hurt us."

"I was ashamed to call my family and ask for help, so I stayed on the streets."

While on the streets of Hollywood and in Downtown Los Angeles, Virginia became addicted to illegal drugs, was violently attacked and experienced intense shame and isolation. Fear of her abusive spouse kept her on Skid Row, "I went where he would never find me. I went to Skid Row because I knew he would never look here. I did it all in fear. I was living in a war zone."

"A homeless woman is victimized more often, and in more ways, than a man. Women tend to get arrested more often than men."

I got arrested a lot. And I got comfortable with that. When you go to jail, you have a bed, you have a meal. They even give you a job. "After a final arrest, Ginger was assigned to the Salvation Army's Safe Harbor 90-day drug treatment program, located in Central City East (Skid Row.)" It was crazy and hard to stay sober on Skid Row. I could see it and smell it." She began to understand that she had a choice, "I realized that I could choose to be a victim or a survivor, and I wasn't going to be a victim anymore. A victim believes that they don't deserve anything, that they're not worthy at all. They're thankful for a breath of air. I decided that people had reached into the depths of hell and pulled me out and that I was going to overcome. I knew that no one was going to do it for me. I would have to do it myself."

Virginia moved into SRO Housing's Angelus Inn--a permanent sober-living site. The Angelus Inn offered a support system and a safe environment where she could begin putting her life back together. She volunteered and worked part-time. She began to attend school, completing a Certificate in Drug and Alcohol Counseling. She learned how to manage her panic disorder through cognitive behavioral therapy. "I even had the opportunity to thank the police officer who arrested me and saved my life."

Virginia's academic journey began when she realized she needed additional skills.

VIRGINIA REED

"I knew I could be anything I wanted to be, but I had to ask myself, who is that person?"

Driven by her desire to give back to those who had helped her and her belief in the 'person in environment' philosophy of Social Work, Virginia reflects on her sobriety and her success.

"What's behind is over and yet I didn't get where I am by myself. I had the support of my neighbor, my hotel manager, my teachers, SRO Housing staff and especially my mentor, Ervin Munro. There is a sense of community on Skid Row that feeds my roots. I have a home and a stake in the neighborhood."

Her work at SRO Housing Corporation is clearly the driving passion in Virginia's life. Beyond her commitment to the organization and the community, Virginia enjoys jetting across the country to visit her family. She has a brother and sister in Denver; her mother lives in Arizona; and her son, daughter and grandchildren live in Florida.

In 2010, life seemed full of possibility. Virginia was awarded Employee of the Year by SRO Housing Corporation and had decided to pursue a Ph.D. to teach at the University level. She was already teaching as a Field Instructor for an MSW/BSW Internship Program and was serving as a supervisor for a Public Ally Program. She was considering doctoral programs when she was diagnosed with breast cancer. "I was diagnosed on Valentine's Day with inflammatory breast cancer. The cancer was growing rapidly and it was metastasizing. It was very scary." Her fear was not just for herself. "I was in a panic. I had an urgent need to accomplish. There was so much I wanted to do for SRO Housing."

IT ALL BEGINS WITH A HOME

Virginia approached cancer in the same way she approached her work, with a plan. "It was very important to me to work." She scheduled grueling chemotherapy treatments around her work week and slowed down only when the cancer required a mastectomy followed by surgery to remove lymph nodes. Her treatment included more chemotherapy and Herceptin infusions and targeted radiation "It's a lot, but you just get up every day and go on."

Despite conquering cancer and all that she has achieved, Virginia still struggles to take credit for her accomplishments.

"I don't do anything alone. Everything I do here at SRO Housing is made possible by others on the staff. I believe everyone has greatness in them."

"Everyone is capable," says Virginia as she tackles daily challenges to meet the needs of SRO Housing residents. She has no plans to slow down. She is seeking a Ph.D. program for working professionals and with her partner of 11 years; Virginia is beginning to envision a life beyond Skid Row. "We are saving for a house and looking forward to living together."

**"Cancer delayed me.
Now, I'm moving forward again."**
Virginia Reed

ROGER ANDERSON

From Hobo to Home

**"I ran away from home when I was 13, in 1979.
I've lived outside since then."**

As a young teen, Roger first settled under a bridge in Florida, selling fish he caught in the river to survive. Later, he set out on foot, following the crops from Florida to California. He has walked the Lewis and Clarke Trail and the Appalachian Trail, "Though I don't much care for that one. They don't have enough storm shelters set up along the way." Roger is restless, always moving, always on the move.

His legs bounce with nervous energy, his hands shake as they comb through neatly trimmed prematurely grey hair. He has climbed mountains, crossed deserts, encountered bears, mountain

IT ALL BEGINS WITH A HOME

Photo by Allen Schaben, *Los Angeles Times*

lions and sea lions. He enjoys an annual trek on the Pacific Coast Trail to San Francisco.

"I take the bus from Skid Row to Thousand Oaks. I catch the trail there; walk up the coast to San Francisco. I walk across the Golden Gate Bridge, turn around and come right back."

From his wooded camp at the edge of a freeway, he walked the streets of Los Angeles ferreting recyclables from trash bins as well as the occasional discarded meal. "It isn't something you'd want to do, but you have to survive. My schizophrenia and my anxiety make it hard for me to stay in one place. Something just tells me to go. Now I have medication, and I am working real hard to stick this out."

"I want to have a home. I've never wanted anything so much in my life before."

Roger was profiled in a *Los Angeles Times* article that followed him on his last day of homelessness and chronicled his move into his new apartment at the Gateways Apartments just before Thanksgiving 2013.

Once Roger settled in to his new home, he was concerned about the adjustment. The isolation of living indoors troubled him.

ROGER ANDERSON

It was too quiet. He spent several nights at his former encampment to calm his nerves. Gradually, he was able to find comfort in his new home. He had help. As with all SRO Housing residents, Roger receives on-site supportive services including the watchful work of a Case Manager who checks in on Roger regularly to ensure his needs are met.

Roger now proudly invites guests to his home to show off items purchased with his monthly disability check; a new brown couch, coordinating rugs, end tables, an entertainment center and music CDs. He has traded a few hours of work at a local business for framed wall art. Every penny has been dedicated toward improving his apartment to personalize it and make it feel more like home.

> **"Can you believe it? Does it look like a real home or what?"**

Roger has purchased new shoes, new outfits and new T-shirts.

> **"And next week, I get teeth!"**

His teeth, badly damaged in a brutal attack years ago, had to be extracted to prepare for a set of dentures. "I love to eat vegetables. That's one thing I have really missed." With his new teeth, he'll finally enjoy a fresh carrot in his well-stocked modern kitchen at the Gateways Apartments.

After years of collecting bottles and cans for recycle, Roger has been able to access Social Security disability funds that provide him a monthly check for rent and groceries and medical care. He has been able to schedule a much-needed surgery for a recurring hernia which his doctor attributes to repeatedly bending over the edge of dumpsters to reach cans and bottles to recycle. That had been Roger's only source of income and remains part of his daily routine, so his doctor gave Roger a long-armed clamp to make it easier for him.

Roger's natural charm inspires offers of help. With Roger's input, SRO Housing's CEO Anita Nelson helped him select a plant to remind him of his former encampment. He felt safe there in the foliage alongside the freeway and the gift was an important step to creating his own home. His on-site Case Manager later helped Roger re-pot the plant that now flourishes, nearly ceiling-high.

In addition to the support he receives at SRO Housing Corporation, Roger has established a bond with Allen Schaben, the *Los Angeles Times* photojournalist who chronicled his move from homelessness to housed. Allen spent three days and nights with Roger, including his last night in the secluded encampment at the edge of the freeway. Allen has made it a habit to visit Roger regularly, bringing practical gifts of toilet tissue and cleaning supplies, and urging Roger to join him for fried chicken lunches.

> "He's a great guy. I don't want him to buy me lunch.
> I don't want him to think I'm using him. But he insists,
> so we go. He's here a lot. I'm glad of that."

Roger seems surprised at his new life. He is learning to relax and enjoy the comforts of a real home.

> "Why is SRO so good to me? I have never been happier.
> I was always afraid to hope for things to be this good."
> **Roger Anderson**

KYOUNG WON

The Art of Survival

From her home in the Brownstone Apartments, Kyoung Won takes a short walk each week to ease her pain through painting. She paints with SRO Housing's Art Workshop each Tuesday afternoon with artist Lillian Calamari at the Rivers Apartments. Kyoung is a talented impressionistic painter and classic Korean calligrapher.

Quiet and intensely private, Kyoung prays for relief from chronic pain, incessant noise from an insomniac neighbor and the busy street beneath her 2nd floor window. Her Catholic faith and her spiritual life are important to her and provide solace.

IT ALL BEGINS WITH A HOME

Her journey to Skid Row has crossed continents. Leaving behind a career as a journalist, she escaped a difficult marriage and left two young sons in Korea to follow her heart to Germany.

There she married a high level professional, "I loved him so much. I married him."

Her second husband was dangerously abusive. Despite her pastor's insistence that she report the abuse to the local German police, she was afraid her husband's position would put her at a disadvantage. Instead of reporting him, she ran.

"One day, I survived and I was so scared. I have only one life. I made an excuse and I went to Korea and then came to Los Angeles. I am safe."

She found work in a Korean-owned dry cleaner but when that job ended, her undocumented status stood in the way of finding new employment and she became homeless. Her circumstances and inability to travel caused a rift with her now-grown sons. They became embittered that she had left them behind. Smiling photographs of them and of her grand-children remind her of better days.

Despite her sadness, she fills her time with art and beauty. She sews quilts, clothing and accessories and she paints. Her walls are adorned with her works, and with a certificate commending her talent from the City of Los Angeles. One of her paintings hangs at City Hall and another graces the wall of SRO Housing's CEO Anita Nelson a gift from Kyoung.

"It is not my style to take from others, I want to give."
Kyoung Won

SANDRA VALENTINE

Carry My Life on My Back

"I left with the clothes on my back. Domestic Violence pushed me into homelessness."

Sandra Valentine is thoughtful and articulate, with a twinkle in her eye that has not been dimmed by a dramatic escape from abuse. Her childhood hurts, caring for an alcoholic mother and witnessing her parents' tumultuous marriage, came full circle when her husband's drinking escalated to violence.

"I thought love would solve everything. It didn't."

"He took a cane and cracked me in the face and broke my jaw. He pushed me back in a chair and strangled me."

IT ALL BEGINS WITH A HOME

Despite restraining orders, he stalked her at work until she lost her job, attacked her repeatedly and abused her emotionally and verbally until she was at a breaking point. "I was despondent. I could not function, could not speak. I checked myself into emergency mental health. And then I got out."

"I asked, 'Why me?' And yet, I did not succumb."

When you are homeless, you sleep wherever you might find shelter.

I went to so many places and programs where they promised housing and it did not come true.

I did not give up hope."

Sandra moved in to her new home at SRO Housing Corporation the Gateways Apartments in 2013.

She smiles, her earrings sparkling,

"Here I am. I chose hope."

She treasures a desk she was able to keep safe in storage through her years of homelessness. "I lost many things to homelessness. Now I have a home."

"I no longer have to carry my life on my back."

Sandra Valentine

DARIUS COFFEY

Feeding the Dream

Darius Coffey believes in three things: gratitude, choices, and the power of laughter. "I wear kooky socks, a funny T-shirt. Don't get me wrong, I am serious about my responsibility. We have 310 people in this program. We provide three meals a day, 365 days a year, and I know every single person. I shake their hand; give them a reason to smile."

In SRO Housing Corporation's Food Services Programs, Darius serves more than nutritious meals. He serves as a role model and an inspiration.

"I came through SRO's program.
I lived at the Marshal House Transitional Housing Program. I made it work.

IT ALL BEGINS WITH A HOME

I can show people by my example that there is a way.
There is no time for whining and excuses.

Myself, I never had a childhood.
I grew up in the system: Foster Care, Youth Authority, and Prison. Coming home from prison, I had to be honest with myself.
I had to admit I had nowhere to go."

Darius found his way to Skid Row and enrolled in the Chrysalis Program to develop job search skills, and was on his way. "I didn't just get one job, I got two. A lot of people are looking for that 'dream job.' I'm willing to start where I can and demonstrate my professionalism and work ethic. I want to create opportunities for my own growth."

"When I applied for this job at SRO Housing Corporation, the line was around the block. I told them, 'I see this job as your slogan in action. You are opening the door for me, you are transforming my life.' I am so grateful for the opportunity to give back."

Darius now lives with his three daughters outside of downtown and commutes to work by bus. He can often be seen in a cheerful selection from his vibrant collection of Superman T-shirts. Darius has been recognized for excellence both at SRO Housing and in the community. He was selected to receive the 2014 Chrysalis Butterfly Award.

He continues to inspire us with his commitment to our mission.

> "I feel proud that my hard work
> has contributed to all that
> SRO Housing does,
> and that includes the Gateways Apartments.
> All of us, together, we built that!"
> Darius Coffey

CHRIS

A Place Where People Love You

"It seems insignificant but simply with a smile, we can change someone's life. We can provide more than a home. We can provide a sense of belonging."

"I never felt that I belonged. I know what it feels like to not have people that love you. That is one of the many things that can lead to homelessness. It can be financial or material. It can be burning bridges; or illness or isolation; or just not feeling like you are good enough."

IT ALL BEGINS WITH A HOME

Chris has served for several years as an SRO Housing Property Manager, responsible for 96 units—including units reserved for chronically homeless persons who have mental illnesses. He is soft-spoken, with soft brown eyes that brighten when he spots and waves to a resident walking past his office window.

> **"I was unwanted and I was homeless as a child from a very young age. Homelessness is more than not having a place to go. It is not having a place where people love you and care about you."**

Chris finds strength in his relationship with God, "I was lost in the wilderness. In my case, God was an integral part of finding who I am. I found a purpose for living. I forgot my own problems and learned to reach out to be beneficial to others. I see the pain and hurt of others. It is not all about me. I was able to overcome the hurt, the pain, the devastation that so many people carry. My relationship with God has taught me to forgive and to let go of the bitterness and anger."

Chris started at SRO Housing as a Desk Clerk and rapidly advanced to a responsible position as Property Manager. He finds meaning in his work for SRO Housing Corporation.

> **"When I get to move someone into a new home, I get to see a life being changed. I see people begin to feel worthy."**

His childhood pain informs his commitment to helping others.

CHRIS

"To be honest, I simply didn't feel loved. I missed out on being connected as a family. That feeling inspires me to connect with others and to help them overcome as I was able to.

"I am grateful and yet, in my eyes, I have not achieved much. I am proud to be in a company where I am surrounded by great people and where every day I have the chance to change someone's life."

Chris

ADDICTION

"Drugs will kill you. There are two ways out, you quit or you die."

George Loftin

DARRIN BROWN

My Life Matters to Me Today

"Living homeless is like a punishment. It is worse than prison."

"At least in prison you have your 'three hots and cot.' You have a roof over your head, food to eat, a place to shower. When I was homeless, I lived with uncleanliness. There were some days, even some weeks that I didn't take a shower. Sleeping with rats, in alleys, in abandoned cars, in abandoned houses, in parks..." Darrin Brown falls silent. He bows his head, shaved clean and gleaming, and presses massive knuckles against his eyes to ward off the memories, "I never want to go back to that." He takes a breath, brightens, and begins again,

IT ALL BEGINS WITH A HOME

"My life matters to me today."

Darrin was homeless from 1986 through 2011. In 1986, he was working for a construction company when he met a woman who introduced him to cocaine. "I got hooked. I lost my job.

I lost my apartment. Since that time, all those years, I was either in jail or in prison or on the streets, chronically homeless. I lived in vacant houses, in parks, any place I could."

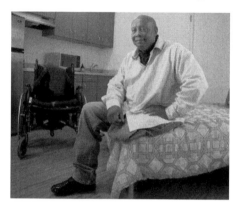

He was also actively involved in drugs, "and doing all sorts of things. It caught up with me. On July 2nd, 1992 I lost my leg. I got shot in both legs. Then I got a severe infection and I was on antibiotics for months. My parents let me come live with them while I recovered. I was shocked because I didn't even know where they lived.

"The way I had been living was indecent. We had lost touch. They took me in, but even after that something just pulled me back into the streets."

To look at Darrin today, it is clear that must have been a powerful pull. Even in a wheelchair, with his left pants leg folded neatly under him, Darrin sits tall, remarkably sturdy.

"It was horrible, horrible."

"Alcohol and drugs go hand in hand. They were calling to me. I went to the mission in 2008 but I wasn't ready for recovery. I had a little shack. When I wanted shelter, I just went to sleep there, sleeping with the rats. I noticed that once people come here to Skid Row, they stay here. In 2011, I was ready. I was feeling the cold. I went to the Midnight Mission and I was there for twenty-six months. Sober. I am in recovery now and taking a look at myself and what I have done."

Darrin has reconnected with his family. "My cousin, she wouldn't let me into her house in the past, wouldn't let me even open the gate. Now, my little nieces and nephews like to visit with me. I keep coins in my pockets, buy them little treats. I'm good for that."

He shakes his head, wondering at the changes in his life.

"I am blessed. I am in adult school, studying for the GED. I read books. I want to go to college. I listen to jazz music. I am interested in the culinary arts."

A bone condition in his remaining leg makes it impossible to stand for more than a few moments, so he has considered studying to be a nutritionist.

"My future looks pretty promising."
Darrin Brown

ROBERT BROWN

Connection is Central

"In your addiction there is a connection with the people you get high with and then there is a connection with those in recovery."

Robert Brown is a solemn man with meditative eyes and a palpable sense of calm. A former teacher whose career succumbed to crack cocaine addiction, he is now a recovery professional and is a graduate of SRO Housing's Veterans Transitional Program for homeless veterans in Los Angeles' Skid Row. Brown, in recovery for 18 years, guides others through a court referral recovery program.

IT ALL BEGINS WITH A HOME

"I will always have a job. There is always going to be a drunk or a drug addict."

Brown served four years in the Air Force, then earned a degree in Fine Arts and taught high school in the city of Compton for a decade. He became addicted to crack cocaine, and got high with professionals and peers.

"I don't think you have to hit bottom to want to recover. I never stole, I never hit bottom. I was a functioning addict."

Brown now works in Los Angeles Centers for Alcohol and Drug Abuse (L.A. CADA)'s court-appointed substance abuse treatment and behavioral recovery program. He provides a program titled "A Path to Recovery and Healthy Living." He also facilitates a weekly Project Fatherhood Group for Men in Relationships. Brown takes deep satisfaction in his work, and offers patience and insight to his clients. He is sparing, though, with the time he invests in court-appointed program participants who are just going through the motions. He quotes Ecclesiastes: There is a time for everything, and a season for every activity.

"And it is not everybody's time. I tell them, 'If it is not your time don't waste mine.' A person enters recovery or they don't. I don't play with these guys. I tell them to come when they are ready. The door is always open."

The door to recovery opened to Brown when he was referred to the Veterans Transitional Program at SRO Housing by a homeless services provider on Skid Row. "I went to the Union Rescue Mission Residential Program. They helped me find SRO Vets program. I've kept the connection with SRO Housing. Jeff Proctor was on staff there and we got on really well. I stayed connected over four years." Brown keeps in touch with program staff that helped him just as he does with the clients he serves, "I want to continue the relationship. I just want them to call or come by."

> **"Success is coming to work every day. In this work, you see things in individuals they don't see in themselves. You see the potential, and sometimes it is discouraging. To get a client to complete the program–start to finish–that's a challenge. When it works, it is rewarding. I get a lot out of it."**

Brown was raised on Long Island, New York in the Hamptons. The family home was an airy eight-bedroom house on an acre of land, a short walk to the beach.

> **"When I grew up, there were only a handful of black people. Now music industry folks like P. Diddy have discovered it. It's a different place."**

He was born and spent his early years in Mississippi but the family fled north after two cousins were lynched. Still, he yearns to return to Mississippi, "They don't lynch people there anymore," but his second wife, who is from El Salvador, is not yet convinced.

Brown and his wife, who works with children on the Autism Spectrum, divide their attention between meaningful work and joy in family. Brown is the proud stepfather to three children and has one grandson. "I am proud of my wife and kids."

His wife, he says, "can't fathom me being an addict. Then she sees old friends and she sees the difference." Recovered, employed and happily married, Brown reflects on one nagging regret:

> **"My mother never got to see me well. She died at forty-nine and never saw me clean and sober."**
>
> Robert Brown

MELVIN CRUTCHFIELD

Opened the Door

Melvin Crutchfield had been in California for just a few months, drawn by an invitation from his daughter, when he discovered SRO Housing's Avenues to Work. "I was angry one day, frustrated, walking it off. And I was walking past and I saw the sign on the door that said SRO Housing, 'Avenues to Work.' I just opened the door and walked in."

He not only walked into an educational and employment program that prepares homeless individuals to re-enter the workforce, he took the first step toward leaving a complicated past behind him.

> "I left my children when I became involved in drugs. I was angry. I was afraid of what I might do. It affected my son the most. He cried and cried. I tell him now that I love him and it is still hard for him. He's grown now and he says, 'I'm not going to leave my children like you did.' That burned my heart. I didn't know."

IT ALL BEGINS WITH A HOME

Now, Melvin has found a sense of peace.

"Two years ago, I was in St Louis and I was just out of drug rehab. Right here, right now, at this moment, I am drug-free."

Melvin has been inspired to make significant changes, "For me, I was never a planner. I was always spur-of-the-moment. Now, I have a job and I have a two-year plan. I work at Wal-Mart. I am in a company that is growing. The job is great. The management is great. I have accomplished what I set out to do."

Melvin's sons and daughters are all grown and have children of their own. The family has reconciled, yet Melvin is haunted by regrets.

"I lost those years when they were growing up. I can't get that back. I see a father and son come into the store where I work and they are talking, excited about things. If only I had stayed. I wonder how things would have worked out."

It was Melvin's 37-year-old daughter who inspired him to come to California. "I am here for my daughter. She had never been out of St. Louis. She's a lot of fun. I talk to her a lot these days. Because of the job, I don't see her so often." Both Melvin and his daughter,

MELVIN CRUTCHFIELD

who dreams of a Hollywood career as a Voice-Over actor, have been homeless, sleeping at the missions on Skid Row.

Melvin has found ways to balance his work life and his off-hours, "I'm more relaxed. Now, I can breathe a little bit. I go to Long Beach and I just sit there watching the ocean. It is a place of peace."

Melvin stands out on Skid Row with his sunny disposition, "I am friendly and I attract a lot of people.

"I am in California! I am on the same streets I saw in the movies! When I left St. Louis, my boss said, 'I'm going to miss your happy a**.' He had plans for me. Now, I have a two-year plan for myself."

> **"Every day now, when I wake up, I think,
> 'I got this. I'm good…what's next?"**
> **Melvin Crutchfield**

WESLEY JONES

sidewalk sleeping to Local 409

> "I was a high school athlete, a college graduate and a union member, a carpenter. And yet I drifted off course. I got off track."

Wesley has an easy-going demeanor and a ready smile. His experience with homelessness began when his drinking became unmanageable, "I thought I had it under control. In the end everything went haywire." He lost his job, his family and his self-esteem.

IT ALL BEGINS WITH A HOME

"I was lying, cheating, sidewalk-sleeping, basket-pushing, panhandling. I remember sleeping in an alley on a discarded sofa, in the cold." "Three years ago, I was on parole, I was walking the streets, I was totally homeless. Sometimes I committed crimes to go to jail so I would have a place to sleep. I made bad decisions."

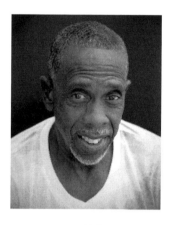

That was before Wesley made a commitment to recovery. He has recently celebrated four years of sobriety and is working towards reinstatement with the carpentry union.

He has reached out to local 409 to work towards rebuilding his career.

He has also reconnected with his family.

"My granddaughter brings tears to my eyes, she's just …wow… she calls me "paw paw."

"Life has gotten much better for me. I am in a joyful place."

Wesley Jones

ALAN GARDENER

Growing a New Life

He does not want his employer to know where he comes from or who he has been.

SRO Housing Corporation's employment development program, Avenues to Work has provided Alan with an opportunity to start over. He was tired and afraid, and ready.

> **"If it wasn't for Avenues to Work, I don't know where I'd be. It feels good when you are alone in the world and someone knows your name and is nice to you. Now, I'm sober and most important, I am working and housed. I'm grateful."**

IT ALL BEGINS WITH A HOME

Alan is quick to point out that he is no different from others on Skid Row who have made mistakes and are trying to do better.

"I'm not unique. I wanted help. I came to the Marshal House. I was fearful that I could lose my housing. I was on GR (General Relief) but I cut myself off from that and saved my money once I started working."

He has decided to be of service, no matter where he is, "I helped a lady across the street," he says solemnly.

He is careful to tally up the help he has received.

"I came in off the street to Avenues to Work. Even the Security Guard was nice to me. Everyone did so much for me, they care about me.

"They helped me get clothes for job interviews. They helped me prepare my resume and helped me get bus tokens to get there. At the Marshal House, my Case Manager goes above and beyond for me. His door is always open for me. The resident manager makes me feel welcomed and the Monday Men's Group helps me out a lot."

SRO Housing Corporation's Avenues to Work partner, Staples Center/AEG, hired Alan. He was one of only 60 applicants selected from nearly one thousand who applied at a Job Fair. Alan was trained and assigned to serve as an Usher. He has proven himself to be a trusted and valued employee. His work ethic and professionalism have impressed his supervisors. Alan has been singled out to staff private receptions and VIP events including the American Music Awards. Celebrities, including Jennifer Hudson and Lenny Kravitz, failed to distract level-headed Alan from his duties.

Alan is happiest when he is called upon to work a sports event. "I am a sports fan. I like the games more than anything else. They keep calling me in to work. They like me." And yet, he is not certain his employer or visiting VIPS would like it if they knew his past.

"I was a Skid Row crack head."

Alan is working hard to rebuild a fractured employment record and reconnect with old friends.

"I was able to clean up some wreckage from my past. I am making payments to the people I owed money to. Its small but they have accepted me back and allowed me to make payments." Family relationships that had suffered from 'worry and fear and disappointment' are on the mend, and Alan is feeling confident.

"I'm growing. I'm on my way to getting my life back."
Alan Gardner

HENRY WALLACE

Money in the Bank

Henry Wallace is lean and long-limbed with the unhurried air of a man at peace with the world. When he sits down for an interview, he is "one hundred days sober with money in the bank." He not only has a plan but the tools to put it in play.

"I have an income. I am not doing desperate things."

A veteran of the Marines, Henry points out that he was a "Peacetime Marine. It was 1983."

Henry came to Avenues to Work after being forced into homelessness when his commercial driving license was suspended due to an alcohol-related incident. After finding his way to Skid Row, Henry found solace, and more trouble, in the bottle. After a night of drinking, while walking on 8th and San Pedro Streets in the pre-dawn hours, he was attacked. "I got stabbed in the neck." He points to a faint scar just above his collar bone, "I could have gotten killed, I 'got gotten.' I have had problems with alcohol in the past. I wasn't aware. It was a wake-up for me."

Since that frightening incident, Henry was motivated to get sober and has found work. "I don't drink any more. That's what got me into this mess."

Avenues to Work helped him get his resume together, and brought him up to date with modern technology. "I didn't know anything about a flash drive." Henry learned not only how to prepare a resume on a computer, and save it onto a flash drive, he learned how to search the internet for jobs and how to conduct himself in interviews. With the help of Avenues to Work, Henry interviewed with a seafood company in Alaska, "I was hired for the whole season. The season is from May to August and typically ends right before Labor Day. The work was wet and cold. There were long hours. But I could work as many hours as I wanted to. I worked 14-16 hours a day. I had a goal."

Henry's goal was to earn enough money to enroll in a vocational training school to follow the natural gas boom to North Dakota. With hard work and discipline, he met his goal before his work assignment with the Alaskan Fish Processing Plant ended and flew back to Los Angeles in early September. "I have sequestered that money." He is staying at a mission and seeking temporary employment until he sets out in February for the Great Plains.

"I'm going to find a job now and then I'm going to get training and a certificate and get in on the fracking industry. I have done my research and I think it looks good. By 2020 they predict that the U.S. will surpass the Middle East in [fossil fuel] production."

Despite the risk of investing in a costly training program with no guarantee of a job, Henry remained optimistic.

"God watches out for me. Living on Skid Row has been an extraordinary experience. They're hiring 8,000 people in North Dakota; I plan to be one of them."

Henry Wallace

GEORGE LOFTIN

A Person Can Change

George Loftin, SRO Housing Corporation 2013 Employee of the Year is a philosopher of the streets. He is a tall man with a long story, a big man in the community, and a well-respected member of SRO staff team.

Standing nearly 7' tall, George is well-known in the Skid Row community. It seems difficult to find anyone who does NOT know George. As he drives an SRO Housing van through the streets of Skid Row, he answers countless shouted greetings and waves with a friendly "Hey hey!"

IT ALL BEGINS WITH A HOME

George knows the Skid Row community inside out.

"A lot of people knew me from the streets. I used to smoke up Los Angeles. I started going downtown thirty-three years ago. Most of my friends from that time are dead. Drugs will kill you. There are two ways out, you quit or you die. I smoked crack so long and yet I bounced back. I changed for the better. People respect that."

George is the middle of three boys, raised in a close family in a strong community. "I grew up in a home with a yard; neighbors would walk to school together. I was fortunate to have my mom and my dad. My mom instilled good qualities in us. I was taught to do things right. My dad was an alcoholic but he was there. I never went hungry. My dad was always bringing home dogs or lizards or possums. He was always promising we'd go hunting. We never did, but my brothers and me, we'd go hunting in the front room. We crawled all around and practiced sneaking up on robbers and thugs. We'd do that for hours."

George played basketball and football at Gardena High School and attended South West College in Los Angeles where he was a stand-out on the school's first football team, before transferring to Arizona University.

"There was nothing I could not do. Even now, after all I've been through, I believe it is important to conduct myself as a decent human being."

Everything changed when his mother passed away. He headed downtown. "I went off the deep end when my mother died. My father passed away more than six years after my mom and I was

GEORGE LOFTIN

already getting loaded then. My little brother was the one who found me. He tricked me. He got me into a locked rehab. I was so angry with him. He brought a birthday cake, German Chocolate cake, my favorite. I was so mad I refused to cut it."

George tried several times to leave drugs behind, but spent long stretches on the streets of Skid Row answering the call of addiction.

"Being homeless, those sidewalks were cold. I was only homeless for two years. I found a hotel where the manager could not collect the rent. I volunteered to collect rent if I could get a place to stay. I got some gangsters to help me. We'd go in there and throw people out. I was the enforcer. I weighed 457 lbs. I told them; 'pay or you'll get hurt.' They paid. I got to keep a portion of the rent. So I had a place to stay and I could get high."

"It's unbelievable how a person can change. It all started when I ran into a pastor I had gone to high school with.

"He came up to me and he said 'We've been looking for you in the neighborhood. We thought you were dead.' He was with the Mission and he wanted me to go into a drug rehab program there. I couldn't say no.

"I was fifty years old. I was scared. I wondered if I could stay clean. Well, I could. It's a blessing."

George first came to SRO Housing Corporation through a Chrysalis referral for Emergency Housing. He now lives at the

IT ALL BEGINS WITH A HOME

Yankee Apartments, an SRO Housing Corporation rehabilitation project that transformed a blighted bar into 80 brand new apartments.

"Now that I work with SRO Housing, I love to come to work."

"I treat everyone equal. I care about people, I talk to them, try to help them out. I buy extra sleeping bags and stuff and I give them out to people living on the street. Only thing is they have to promise not to sell them. They say I make them feel human. The bad stuff I've done, I don't glorify it. That's in the past."

He enjoys time with his brothers and their families, sharing meals and recipes handed down from their mother, including homemade barbecue sauce, apple pie and lemon meringue pie. His marriage had ended, and yet his recovery from addiction brought his ex-wife and daughter back into his life.

"We have a good relationship. I am so proud of my daughter. She was an athlete in high school. I went to all her games. Now, she's a coach at Torrance High School and I still go to all her games. She is a beautiful person. When I got the Employee of the Year award, it almost brought tears to my eyes. I showed it to my daughter and she told me,

" 'You were doing your best, just like you always told me to do.' "

LAMONT REYNOLDS

The Devil Steps In

"It was hard, being homeless, in the rain, living against a building, living in fields…"

Lamont Reynolds remembers how rough it was on the streets where he made a meager living by recycling cans and bottles culled from downtown trash bins and sidewalk discards.

"I was on the street. It was humiliating."

Lamont now lives at the Florence Hotel, where he has settled in. "I'm proud of getting a roof over my head and keeping it. It's better than being outside on that sidewalk. It took me a long time. I'm blessed for Shelter Plus Care."

He graduated from a drug treatment program and from a job training program, landed a job and then was laid off. He is holding

IT ALL BEGINS WITH A HOME

tight to hope and to sobriety. "Most of the people I was with there in the program, I see them back out on the streets again."

Lamont was born and raised in Los Angeles and drugs seemed to offer comfort when a string of deaths in his family left him reeling. "There was one death after another, my mom, my dad, my sister." It wasn't long before he was strung out.

He was once a family man, with a wife and five children. Now, he is learning the lessons he worked to teach them.

"There were a lot of things I had to learn. I wouldn't take care of my bills. I didn't know how. I had my wife take care of the bills. I had kids and I have grandchildren. I taught them, 'Always depend on yourself. Get out and get on your own.' And there I was, homeless and addicted, and I had to deal with jail and things. "I wish I didn't have that addiction. It's not gone. I still get urges. Out there on the streets, I didn't have to pay rent. I had money in my pocket. If I got bored, I'd go do drugs. I knew it was wrong. Even now, if I leave that spot open, the devil steps in."

While living temporarily with a sister, Lamont was picked up once again by police. The sentencing judge had seen Lamont before and offered him another chance by sending him to mandatory drug treatment.

Lamont was grateful, "I knew I was finally going to get help."

"Now, it's up to me to pay my rent. I don't want any violations on my housing record. If I get evicted, it takes a long time to get back in. I look at life. I can't change things. I can't think I'm better than anybody. I'm the same person," says Lamont.

> **"Having a home and a roof over my head everything has been good. I am happy. I'm blessed."**
> **Lamont Reynolds**

MARK DEAN SOUKUP

A Lot More of Everything

The television and movie industry is a fast-moving business and Mark Dean Soukup kept pace with the help of drugs. His income made it possible to afford an expensive drug habit while amassing a collection of cars, a home, and a substantial bank account.

When he was diagnosed with a dangerous heart condition, hospitalized and near death, his girlfriend took advantage of his illness. She looted his assets and emptied his bank accounts of hundreds of thousands of dollars.

> **"I was amazed at how quickly it happened.
> In a way, it did me a favor. I had way too much stuff."**

IT ALL BEGINS WITH A HOME

Now, his health has improved, he has made peace with the past and is adjusting to a simpler life. Mark is an early riser and makes coffee every morning in the community kitchen for his neighbors at the Florence Hotel.

"It is fulfilling. It takes a lot less to make me happy now. I try to help people. Lots of people here have lost everything. I had more, so I've lost a lot more of everything."

Mark's fragile health, persistent pain and a balance disorder have made it difficult to find work despite his desire to make good on a locksmith training course he recently completed. He takes medication and works with a Mental Health Therapist for depression, anger and what he refers to as 'suicide issues.' He also finds solace in books.

"I am a voracious reader. I read mystery novels, crime novels, history. I read at least three books a week and I enjoy the luxury of having the library just up the street. I don't drink, I don't smoke and I no longer do drugs, so I need some sort of challenge. Back in the day, I tested with a pretty decent IQ."

Mark was born in Milwaukee to parents who ultimately proved to be dramatically mismatched. His mother was a war-bride, a survivor of tragedy who lost her immediate family in the Hiroshima bombing. She was swept off her feet by his father, a post-war occupation forces soldier. The family settled in the mid-west and later relocated to Los Angeles following his father's flourishing career as a corporate executive. "I was a child of privilege. I always had money and could do as I pleased."

MARK DEAN SOUKUP

Mark's mother has passed away and his father now lives with Alzheimer's disease in a care facility. "My family is no longer a part of my life," he sighs.

Mark looks towards the community room window where the Florence Hotel abuts the streets of Skid Row, "I have considered what it would take to survive or to end my life. I am not a 'woe is me' type. I am very practical. I take pride in my situation. I live within my means. I pay my rent the very first day of each month. I saved a bit and bought myself a small TV and a laptop. Sometimes my health issues make it so I can hardly stand up and walk but I make it a point every day to present myself to my neighbors, to smile, say hello."

Mark came to SRO Housing Corporation through a referral for recovering substance abusers, "Thankfully my counselor recommended the Marshal House drug rehabilitation program."

"I am extremely grateful for all SRO Housing has done for me. I am reassured that my inner situation, my values and morals are in the right place. I am content and I am very appreciative of the help I have received here."
Mark David Soukup

JEFFREY OWENS

Others Can Too

Jeffrey Owens is a titanic of a man, taller than the stainless steel refrigerator in the newly refurbished kitchen of the Golden West Hotel, and as solid as the cast iron pots on the gleaming new double-wide industrial range. He is a physically commanding presence, broad shouldered, beefy, head and shoulders above everyone in the room, and yet he moves with the tentative carefulness of someone afraid to plunge through thin ice to the drowning depths below.

The depths of alcohol addiction are a darkly familiar place to Jeffrey. When he tried to escape the squalor of the streets to the safety of a secret corner in his mother's garage, his hulk and the noise he made, soon gave him away. With few choices and nowhere to turn, he begged his siblings for help. They directed him to services on Skid Row, where they assured him he would get the help, and the housing, he needed to rebuild his life.

IT ALL BEGINS WITH A HOME

Jeffrey moved from a sobriety program at the Los Angeles Mission to SRO Housing's Emergency Housing Program at the Panama Hotel before settling in to a new life at the Golden West  Hotel one year ago. As with every man and woman residing in the building at the time, he decided to stay put during renovation. The building is one of SRO Housing Corporation's longest-serving properties, opened in 1988, and dedicated to individuals living with mental health and substance abuse disorders.

Together with his neighbors, Jeffrey watched as the well-worn building was transformed from a Transitional Housing Program, with a maximum stay of two years, into Permanent Supportive Housing.

Now, in addition to the sleek contemporary spaces of the completed renovation, the building boasts expanded capacity with four offices turned into additional private permanent supportive housing units.

Jeffrey is one of 44 men and 10 women currently living at the Golden West. All have access to on-site supportive services including case management, life skills services and socialization and recreation activities. Jeffrey enjoys gathering in the newly refurbished community room with his neighbors to play dominos and board games.

He stands quietly in the roomy, fully renovated kitchen, smiling gently as he recounts highlights of the transformation and the highs and lows of his life.

He credits his family, the LA Mission and SRO Housing for helping him. "I was carrying the load for some time. It wasn't me. It was an addiction. I am sober now and I am on medication. Tragic things happened. It wasn't my choice," he says earnestly.

Jeffrey is grateful for the help he has received, grateful for the opportunity to start over, and thankful for the upbeat support of his family, "They encourage me. We get on the phone and we chop it up a bit." He continues to attend classes at the LA Mission and attends church regularly.

He describes his journey to housing at the Golden West, "I went to the Russ Hotel and I had fear in my heart. I didn't know what was going to happen." He completed the necessary paperwork and within hours had been called and welcomed to his new home,

"I have a nice big room and the new kitchen on the first floor."

Jeffrey has begun to explore the joys of independent living; buying groceries, cooking himself meals in the community kitchen, and cleaning up afterwards. "I want to keep the kitchen nice and clean. When you're drinking on the streets, you'd rather drink your money up than buy food. You just starve and then you eat off any cart that comes by handing out free food. Sometimes it's spoiled and it makes you sick. I've been sick many times. Not now. I can have my own food. Tonight before bed, I'm going to have a big bowl of cereal with cold milk. It helps me sleep well." His face blossoms into a bright smile and as Jeffrey straightens his broad shoulders, he looks blissfully happy.

> **"Sometimes people dream, and those dreams come true.
> I did it, and I know there are followers after me.
> Someone else is behind me, and he can do it too."**
> Jeffrey Owens

JIM THOMPSON

Walking the Distance

Jim Thompson has walked the streets of Skid Row for decades. Starting in 1971 when he was a letter carrier and delivered mail to SRO Housing Corporation offices and continuing today as he walks, slowed by lung disease, through the community that has been his home since 1995.

He takes a moment to glance out the window of the community room in the Florence Hotel. It is SRO Housing Corporation's first residential property and the home where Jim has settled in and started over. The streets of Skid Row roil beyond the window. Traffic hums, a near-constant westward flow, the sidewalk is crowded with loiterers: drug users, hustlers and street-dwellers as well as a promenade of community members from nearby service providers. Inside, it is quiet and Jim is in a thoughtful mood.

IT ALL BEGINS WITH A HOME

"For more than twenty years, I carried mail while I was smoking drugs. Cocaine was my drug of choice. When you're down here, you get what's available here. It's walking distance, you get it."

Jim admits that the deepest regret of his life was the end of his career with the postal service, "My union was trying to help, but when you're a user, you don't care. They fought for my job but I started using again and I couldn't go back. I gave up. I retired at 55. It was not what I wanted to do. I felt so bad about that. By the grace of God, I was never arrested. I'm proud of never having been in jail."

Instead, Jim spent years imprisoned by his drug habit, using during the day and sleeping in Skid Row missions at night, "I didn't have a place to be during the day but I never, not one time, I never slept on the streets. I didn't want to have someone coming up and killing me. Sleeping in the mission was bearable. I had a roof over my head, I had a bed. I didn't mind sleeping with a lot of people as long as we weren't in the same bed."

He struggled through failed attempts at sobriety and shudders at the memory of the state he was in when his family found him to inform him of a death in the family.

"I would have lived on the streets and died there but my daughter and my ex-wife came looking and found me."

Finally, he was ready to make a change. He spent a winter at SRO Housing's Panama Hotel in the cold weather program, then moved to the Florence Hotel where he has been ever since. "It's better than being out there. I haven't used for nine years. I stopped smoking cigarettes too. I have a lung disease, COPD."

Jim pauses to catch his breath before shuffling down the hall to climb a short flight of steps from the community kitchen and TV room to his room on the 2nd floor where he will place a call to his son later in the day.

"My son still loves me. Now I have a phone and I call him like we're around the corner. I never alienated myself from my family. I would rather die than do anything to hurt them."

Family remains important to him. One of two sets of twins and six children raised by a single mother, Jim puzzles at his son and daughter who have not yet had children, "They're heck when they're little but when they're grown, you want your kids to see you."

It was not always that way. When he was using drugs, he isolated himself from family.

"For me, my Christmas was… I didn't talk to anybody. You do a lot of thinking on Christmas when you're alone in your room. I am not a religious person, but I didn't do this on my own. God helped me. God let me live long enough to get clean."

Jim is enjoying his sobriety with Veterans Administration benefits of Vietnam-era military service in the Air Force. He avoided combat duty by serving in the Philippines and at March Air Force base,

"If you signed up, you didn't have to go to the front lines. I served a full four years. I enjoyed it very much."

Despite his past challenges and ongoing health problems, Jim is enjoying his life at the Florence Hotel, "I have a bad heart, I have COPD and still I have to say I'm feeling a lot better now that I have my VA benefits and I qualified for Social Security."

With a laugh, and a subtle cough, he smoothes the shopping bag at his side, "I got myself some shoes today and I got a haircut." He

IT ALL BEGINS WITH A HOME

plans to slip into the shoes and try them out with a walk down the hallway as he thinks about his goals for the future.

> **"I want to keep living until I get real old
> so they can keep giving me my Social Security money."**
>
> Jim Thompson

ECONOMICS

"I didn't want to take away from my mother. I couldn't help pay the bills, so I went out to the streets."

Thomas Johnson

THOMAS JOHNSON

i'm still Alive

As the oldest son in a single parent home, Thomas was accustomed to shouldering a burden for the family from an early age. He was laid off from his job and his problems with reading and spelling made it difficult to find work. He lost his apartment and moved back in with his mother until shame moved him to the streets. "I didn't want to take away from my mother. I couldn't help pay the bills, so I went out to the streets. At first, it was less stress, not having to support the family. I was just focused on survival."

To Thomas, survival meant "getting beat out of your money, people stealing from you, people trying to hurt you."

"It's rough, it's rough out there. It's like being in the lions' den. But I got accustomed to living on the streets."

IT ALL BEGINS WITH A HOME

Pointing to the stylish blue print shirt he is wearing after completing his application for housing, he says, "This is the only clothes I've got. I have one more pair of pants, but this shirt is it. Being homeless, I'd go to the Laundromat and have to put my clothes back on when they were still a little wet. You get accustomed to it. You learn how to survive."

"Having my own home means a lot to me. I don't have to get up and move. When you're sleeping on the sidewalk, they come and wake you up in the morning before the police come. The police come and they'll give you a ticket if you're still asleep there. You can't pay the ticket, you'll go to jail."

"Having my own place means I can cook my own food. I won't have to stand in a line to get something to eat."

Thomas dreamed of having a home and of spending all his money on food. "I know how to cook, I learned in my mother's kitchen."

He had plans for a Thanksgiving meal, "I want to bake a Cornish hen with cornbread dressing and an apple pie." He also had plans for how having a home would offer simple comforts,

"I would like to get a house phone. When I come home, there will be messages waiting for me. And then, I'll cook a nice, good dinner."

Thomas moved into his new home at the Gateways Apartments in November of 2013.

THOMAS JOHNSON

"It seems like a little thing, but now, I can watch TV and be able to hear it. They had TV in a lot of places, but you sat in the lobby and you try to hear the TV over all that noise, you got accustomed to it, but you couldn't really enjoy it.

"When you're on the streets, you don't sleep all that well. Having my own place means I can close the door and enjoy a good night's sleep on a bed."

Thomas Johnson

ETHEL KORMAN

Fine, Just Fine

Ethel Korman is celebrating her 3rd year as a resident of SRO Housing Rosslyn Hotel in downtown Los Angeles. She is one of only a handful of residents who opted to stay during renovations of the units and a full-scale historic preservation of the lobby and mezzanine of the 1923 Beaux Arts building as it is being transformed into affordable housing for low-income and homeless residents.

> **"I used to dread coming downtown, I had lived in Hollywood for a long time. But it has been fine, just fine."**

Ethel has a wistful quality, her voice softens and she repeats the final words of her sentences in a soothing refrain. She sits in the filtered sunlight of her upper floor apartment in the building as sirens wail below and the dull *thunk* of ongoing construction reverberates

IT ALL BEGINS WITH A HOME

from down the hall. Her hair frames her face in soft wisps and she squints behind thick wire-framed eyeglasses.

Several years ago, she lost her job and her failing eyesight made it impossible to find new work. At first, credit cards seemed to offer a solution. Until she realized she could not pay.

"It bothers me that I had financial issues. I got in trouble with credit cards and I was evicted from my apartment. I wish it hadn't been that way."

She was scared. The first thing she did was to call her older brother and was shocked when he refused to take her in. Then, she tried asking friends.

"I had no place to go, no place."

She had been forced to flee from a life she had become accustomed to. It seemed a refrain of her late mother's struggles. Her mother, a Polish immigrant, was a World War II refugee and a Holocaust survivor who had started over in the United States only to be widowed with two young children when Ethel was five years old. Her brother was sickly, and her mother moved the family to Los Angeles from Philadelphia on a doctor's recommendation.

"She survived and so have I," muses Ethel. She admits she would have preferred to stay in West Hollywood but soon realized she had no choice. She finally arranged an invitation to move in with her adult son and his family out of state. It soon proved to be a mistake. She missed the sunlight, the warm climate and the pace of life in the city. If only she could find some place that would accept her cat and that she could afford on her limited income.

ETHEL KORMAN

"I came back to Los Angeles and I stayed in a motel until I found this place. Finances drove me here."

When she moved in to her 11th floor unit at the Rosslyn Hotel, she was grateful for the affordable rent. The hubbub of the city bothered her at first, "I had some sleepless nights with the noise of the sirens and the people on the streets below. I have learned to turn the fan on to cancel out the noise." She has also come to appreciate the convenience of the location. A variety of public transportation options are just steps from her door and the public library is a short walk away.

"I have a small apartment here, it is compact. I can afford to live here."

"When they came to say they were going to be doing renovations, as much as the relocation money sounded terrific, really terrific, I realized it was not going to work. And now I'm back in my fixed-up apartment. They made it nice."

"It worked out fine, just fine."
Ethel Korman

LIBRADA PORTER

Principal of Enjoying Life

Librada Villanueva-Porter is in love with her life on Skid Row. The love of her life, Mr. Porter, moved them to Skid Row when he lost his job in 2001. Because all SRO Housing Corporation properties are Single Room Occupancy, meaning only one person per unit, the Porters lived across the hall from one another.

Ms. Porter has never been homeless. Like many of SRO Housing Corporation's longest residents, she is a low-income retiree. She feels at home in the community.

"It is exactly like living at home with a large family."

A native of the Philippines, Ms. Porter holds a Masters Degree in Education and before relocating to the United States she worked as the Principal of a school and founded a Pre-School.

IT ALL BEGINS WITH A HOME

Her family, all in the Philippines, includes eleven brothers and sisters as well as adult twin sons from an earlier marriage. Both teach at Community Colleges. Her husband, Mr. Porter is now confined to a convalescent home in Pomona and Ms. Porter travels hours by bus each week to visit him.

"I am fearful that my husband may not make it. But for now, I am just going to enjoy life to the maximum and share my blessings with other people."

With the sunny disposition of an early childhood educator, Ms. Porter makes a point of sharing lessons on life in her surroundings.

"If I die when I am 80 or 90 years old, I will think, 'What a short good life.' I have been surrounded by community.

"Being here is not much different from living with family because we have a strong community here in Skid Row."

Ms. Porter, who describes herself as a "happy good fellow," is active as a volunteer for SRO Housing Corporation events, always eager to be a part of the action. Her ebullience is infectious,

"She lights up the room wherever she goes," says SRO Housing Corporation Seniors Program Manager Victor Constantino. Ms. Porter was among a large group of volunteers who helped to greet and guide guests at the grand opening of SRO Housing's the Gateways Apartments in November 2013 and she looks forward to her next opportunity to help.

Ms. Porter regularly volunteers for the City of Los Angeles Department of Aging and is active in SRO Housing Art Workshops at the Rivers Hotel taught by artist Lillian Calamari. Her artwork has been displayed at Los Angeles' Barnsdall Art Park and at Los Angeles City Hall.

"I always want to be there to help anyone, any time."
Librada Porter

IT ALL BEGINS WITH A HOME

Ms. Porter and fellow Harold Hotel resident, Mr. Thomas, at SRO Housing Corporation Resident Appreciation Day 2012

MCKINLEY THOMAS

Put a Nickel Aside

Mr. McKinley Thomas has lived at SRO Housing Corporation's Harold Hotel for 24 years.

He first came to the community as a child, with an uncle who raised him on Wall Street. Where people now sleep on the streets, there had been single family homes and low-rent apartment houses. He remembers SRO Housing, and the community, as it has changed over the years.

"The James Wood Community Center used to be a Laundromat. I saw all the SRO Housing places being fixed up; the Lyndon, the Ford, the New Terminal, the Rivers, the Yankee.

IT ALL BEGINS WITH A HOME

Then they built the Gateways...brand new."

"I know some SRO staff from way back. A lot of people you see working at SRO Housing, I've seen them drunk and high when they could hardly get around out there. SRO Housing turns their life around. They have to get themselves started, then SRO Housing gives them a job and they have a position, they have something to live for."

Mr. Thomas' apartment is warm and filled with south facing light. It serves as a shrine of sorts. The walls are covered with framed Certificates of Appreciation and Achievement from SRO Housing Corporation, The Department of Aging, Chrysalis, The City of Los Angeles, to name just a few. Plaques and awards include a Tenant Appreciation Award. A folding wheelchair is tucked behind the entry door and a walker is parked outside in the hallway.

A prized collection of SRO Housing Corporation uniforms hang near the door, including one emblazoned with "Volunteer."

"It would be hard to say what my life might have been without SRO Housing. I'm happy. I am content."

Family photographs line the bookshelves and share space in scrapbooks that overflow with photographs and memorabilia related to SRO Housing. He first came to SRO Housing for help with low-income housing, "I've never been a money-maker. I was on GR (General Relief)."

Mr. Thomas, 'everyone calls me Mr. T.' was hired to work for SRO Housing Corporation, first as a Janitor and later as a Dining Center Worker. In recent years, after his retirement, he took pride in volunteering to cook for the Resident Appreciation Day events.

MCKINLEY THOMAS

Mr. Thomas has developed close friendships among his neighbors at the Harold Hotel and in the community. The chaos of the street below his 2nd floor window overlooking the James Wood Community Center and San Julian Park does not concern him.

"Whatever happens out there, I'm not out on the streets. I'm on a different page as them out there on the street. If I'm out there, I'm on my way somewhere; to go visit my family, to go shopping, just passing through on my way somewhere. I go to Santa Monica. I go to Long Beach to eat fish. I get out."

His many years as a Dining Center Worker in SRO Housing's Food Program set an example for his now-grown sons, both of whom are professional chefs. One son lives in Los Angeles and one has his own restaurant in Las Vegas. "They took after me, they love to cook." He cooks for himself each day in a tidy kitchenette that lacks only an oven for baking, "I love to bake. Chocolate cake is my favorite. And lemon meringue pie."

Mr Thomas is comfortable in his home and waves away his family's repeated requests to move away from Skid Row.

"I'm not going anywhere. SRO gives people a chance. They helped out a lot of people. When people work for SRO Housing, they know they'll be looked after. Low Income Housing helped me put a nickel aside now and again. It has been very beneficial to me."
McKinley Thomas

HORACE HIGGINS

Writing with Heart

Horace Higgins lives at SRO Housing Corporation's Harold Hotel and spends his days writing stories that bring to life raw truths from the streets.

Mr. Higgins is confident and intense. "I am an artist. I want my work to be informative and entertaining," he says. In addition to his daily discipline of writing, he commutes regularly to Cedars Sinai Hospital for cardiac therapy as he recovers from open-heart surgery.

He was born in Durham, North Carolina, one of ten children and grew up in extreme poverty.

He was raised by his mother.

"My father just didn't have the heart to stick around."

IT ALL BEGINS WITH A HOME

Horace left home at 17 with an 8th grade education, a driving creative passion and a curiosity about the world beyond his humble beginnings.

His first stop was Washington D.C. where, in 1975, he first started writing. He has traveled through a colorful career that has included writing poetry, writing and producing jingles for radio advertising, producing television commercials, as well as managing and producing singers and even cutting a successful record on his own record label.

After a move to New York City and a divorce, he resettled in Los Angeles in 1989, and was eager to launch a career in screenwriting. He enjoyed brushes with success. When a potential production deal fell through, he was devastated. "The next thing I knew, I was on the outside looking in. I wasn't invited to the meetings. Time was dragging on and nothing was happening."

He took odd jobs to survive, but a string of injuries, to a leg and a foot, kept him from working. He had exhausted all his funds and was in a leg cast when he sought help in finding housing. He moved to the Panama Hotel with a housing voucher and later, in the spring of 1992, moved to the Harold Hotel.

At one point, he tried his hand at acting. His acting coach redirected him, "He said, 'You're wasting your time here.' He said I should be writing."

So, Horace turned his full attention to his writing and has never looked back. He has 30 projects in the works spanning a variety of genres, Sci-Fi, True Crime, Thrillers and Love Stories for television, motion pictures and radio. He has written 150 songs and is not shy about crooning a sample lyric or two. Horace is an eternal optimist and is dedicated to building his mastery of technique.

> **"I read books on screenwriting from cover to cover.
> It is very important to have technique.**
>
> **I am good at my craft. I have a comfortable home here; it makes it possible for me to focus on my art."**
> Horace Higgins

DARNELL GUY

Possible to Raise My Kids

Darnell Guy is SRO Housing Corporation's longest-serving staff member, hired in 1985.

He speaks highly of SRO Housing Corporation and our CEO, Anita Nelson.

> "I work out in the field and I may be sweaty and dirty and Ms. Nelson always takes time to listen and to make me feel recognized and important."

Darnell is proud to have had stability in his work and to have survived, "through fires and storms," as he worked in both of the parks developed and managed by SRO Housing Corporation; Gladys Park and San Julian Park.

IT ALL BEGINS WITH A HOME

"Working in the parks is not always an easy day. You get cursed at. You get hollered at. In 1995, I was attacked and I lost my teeth and nearly lost my eye. Sometimes at the end of the day I left with a broken heart. People would come to us and ask for a place to eat or sleep and you couldn't help them all."

The parks have provided a rich variety of experience for Darnell including danger, glamour, and an opportunity to help the community. "I have met actors who filmed in Skid Row at SRO Housing sites and I have met killers who came to Skid Row to hide. In the parks, I would listen to people's problems. You learn to humble yourself. You don't know who people are or where they came from. They once had normal lives like we did. A gentleman who used to sleep in the park, Winston, said he was a mechanic. Now he has his own shop. And a man who used to be on Gladys Street on the sidewalk, he used to hit the pipe. I told him to put that pipe down, 'That's not you,' I said. Two years later, he pulled up in a nice car. I didn't recognize him. He thanked me for encouraging him to give up the pipe. It's not just me. It's SRO Housing. The company gives people a chance to pick themselves up. People came from abuse, from battered lives. They go a long way by helping people."

"You have to be tender hearted. It makes it better to be understanding and kind."

SRO Housing, says Darnell, has helped him. "Ms. Anita Nelson (SRO Housing CEO) made it possible to raise my kids. When I got my divorce, I had to get a night job to pay child support for my girls. She understood. She let me keep my job. She knew I was so tired. She made sure I had a job. I could never run out on her."

DARNELL GUY

"I dedicated part of my life to the company. There were painful moments. SRO Housing helped me when I had to make sacrifices for my family. They helped me raise my family."

"Ms. Trena Rucker (SRO Housing Director of Human Resources) is another beautiful person. She has always looked out for me, always been there to listen. One day, when we got word that Gladys Park was going to close, I didn't know what I was going to do." Darnell remembers with tears welling in his eyes, "I asked Trena Rucker. She calmed me. I felt so relieved."

"I have never been on drugs. I have never been in prison. I've always try to do right. SRO Housing has changed a lot of lives. I thank God I can be a part of that."

Darnell is originally from Long Beach. As a young man, he worked in building maintenance for the owner of a building on Spring Street who introduced him to Andy Raubeson, the founding Executive Director of SRO Housing, who gave Darnell a job at our first SRO Housing property, the Florence Hotel. Darnell remembers his first day with a laugh, "I thought, 'Oh that's an extravagant name,' I didn't know I was going to work in Skid Row. There was a lot of homelessness and a lot of drugs."

IT ALL BEGINS WITH A HOME

(R) Darnell Guy in 1980s

(far right) Darnell Guy 2014, posing next to his name on a past Anniversary poster

Darnell worked first as a Maintenance Worker, then as a Painter. "I learned a lot of trades at SRO Housing. When they got a contract with the City to run Gladys Park, I moved to parks. I did the hardscape and the landscaping. I laid sod and trimmed trees. I learned to pressure wash the sidewalk. I helped to keep the parks safe, to keep drugs and alcohol out of the park. When Anita Nelson came in she made it safe and comfortable to work here."

"A lot of people who work here, they don't know who I am. As a man of my age, I have worked here for so long. I am afraid one day I'll have to retire and move on."

Whenever Darnell moves on, he appears ready to keep busy, "I jog and I eat healthy and I make people laugh and I sing. When I chose to get married, I had four kids to raise, so I just couldn't do the music business. I still use my voice. I love singing and writing and composing music."

"I stayed here because I have peace of mind."

Darnell Guy

History of Transformation

SRO Housing Corporation has a 30-year history of transforming dilapidated properties into clean, safe, contemporary studio apartments.

At the time of this publication, SRO Housing Corporation has developed over 2,300 units of affordable housing and is recognized as the one of the largest developers of housing for homeless and low-income individuals in the Western United States.

IT ALL BEGINS WITH A HOME

TRANSFORMING HOUSING

SRO Housing Corporation offers clean, safe and affordable single room occupancy housing (emergency, transitional and permanent) for homeless and low-income individuals.

While some units consist of a sink, complete furnishings, linens and a refrigerator, others are contemporary studio apartments that include a full-size private bathroom and sleek modern kitchenette. In general, anyone over the age of 18 without a permanent residence and with some form of steady income is eligible to live in an SRO Housing Corporation unit.

Ford Hotel Interior BEFORE

Ford Apartments Interior AFTER

TRANSFORMING HOUSING

SRO Housing serves a community that has a history of welcoming low-income individuals...and an enduring need for transformation.

The Leo Hotel was replaced by newly constructed Renato Apartments in 2010.

IT ALL BEGINS WITH A HOME

TRANSFORMING COMMUNITY

SRO Housing Corporation has developed two parks in the community, Gladys Park and San Julian Park and owns and operates the only Community Center in the Central City East (Skid Row) area of Downtown Los Angeles, the James Wood Community Center, and manages a pocket park for local residents.

James Wood Community Center

SRO Housing has transformed every building on the East side of Wall Street between 5th and 6th Streets in downtown Los Angeles. The calm, clean streetscape appears plucked from an upscale urban neighborhood, but is just steps away from the chaos and despair of Skid Row.

TRANSFORMING LIVES

In 2013, over 500 homeless and low-income individuals stood in line to apply for housing in SRO Housing Corporation's newly constructed Gateways Apartments.

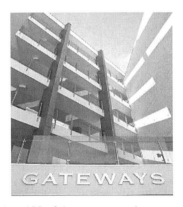 

Today, 108 of those men and women call the Gateways Apartments home.

Where once there was despair, now there is hope.
Where once there was homelessness. Now there is home.

JUSTICE

"My job is about giving back to the community that gave to me when I needed them."

Deborah Martin

GILBERT CORTEZ

Thankful I Got Caught

Gilbert Cortez might look menacing at a glance. A convicted felon, he is a big man with a shaved head, tall and tattooed. He is dressed in what might be seen as gang-issue baggy black clothing. And yet, Gilbert is a sweet-tempered, easy-going fellow. He earns a living with his heft, as a Security Guard. He struggles to resist the temptations of the street.

He has been imprisoned twice and is achingly aware that a third-strike conviction could send him back. "When I was in prison, I came to realize I've done a lot of bad things. I came to realize I was thankful that I got caught for a minor offense. I saw people who were serving 30 to 40 years. A lot of them, when they get out, they go right back. Some have been there so long they don't know how to adjust."

IT ALL BEGINS WITH A HOME

"I could not understand how anyone could get used to being told what to do, showering in a crowd of men, standing in line for food, standing in line everywhere."

Gilbert was the eighth person in line when applications were opened for our Gateways Apartments. He stood in line and slept on the streets for two nights and three blistering-hot summer days to secure a spot among 500 applications submitted. He was determined to change how he was perceived and how his life might move forward.

"I have a bald head. The way I look, I got stopped almost every day.

My name is a common name, it pops up with my convictions, and similar names pop up. It happened a lot. Even when I went out to get groceries, I was getting stopped. I was getting mad. I needed help. So I came here to start over."

Gilbert is struggling with his new surroundings, "I feel I'm at the bottom here on Skid Row. I'm used to living in expensive areas, living the good life. For me, I want to save as much money as possible. I want to get out of here.

I know it's going to be hard. I'm competing against people coming right out of college. I really wanted to go to school but I have to finish my GED first."

GILBERT CORTEZ

Until then, Gilbert continues to work security at a local convenience store and continues to fight temptation.

"I am fighting the urge to sell drugs again. I don't want to take that chance. Here on the streets, there's a lot of drugs. There's trash everywhere and there's fights."

And for Gilbert, there are dreams...

"I think if I can get a job working security for the movies, it would be good. You get to see the actors, you make a good living."
					Gilbert Cortez

CHARLES BIVIANS

A Path From Nothingness

Charles Bivians is a sculptor and painter who compares himself to Rip Van Winkle, "One day I woke up and I was on Skid Row. All those years had gone by."

Years had passed while he was asleep to the rhythms of a cycle that moved him from the street to the justice system, from jailhouse to recovery house and back again.

"And then one day, I just woke up and that urge for drugs was gone. It was just gone."

IT ALL BEGINS WITH A HOME

He had already given up stealing and had begun to recycle cans. He was ready to work towards sobriety. He entered a program and set about redefining himself as a man and as an artist. He drew, painted and sculpted. He carved clay with Popsicle sticks, recycled cans to purchase foundry services to pour molds of sculptures that he then hand-finished. He moved to SRO Housing's the Marshal House, Transitional Housing Program and later moved on. He was living in a cramped hotel with his wife and her daughter when she became pregnant with their son. He was inspired. He painted and drew images of his tall model-thin wife; he was mesmerized by his spirited young son.

When his wife moved and took the children, he mourned but maintained his sobriety. He was evicted from his hotel room and contacted his previous case worker at SRO Housing for help. "I didn't have anywhere to go."

He started over with emergency housing, and after a nine-year absence, moved again into the Marshal House Transitional Housing Program where his Case Manager, Aaron, helped him formulate a plan. He credits the concentration of social services in Skid Row with saving him. His Social Worker, Mike, at the Downtown Mental Health Center taught him to meditate. Learning to quiet the noise of racing thoughts and concerns allowed Charles to climb out of a crushing depression and helped him create. He continued to paint, draw and sculpt and gathered several pieces to display at downtown Los Angeles Art Walk.

"Nobody bought anything."

He had to borrow a friend's truck to move the heavy pieces back to his room. On the way, a polished aluminum bas relief sculpture in the back of the open truck caught the eye of a collector who purchased it for over a thousand dollars. Then, Charles got a phone call. He had been approved for permanent housing at SRO's Renato Apartments. Things were finally coming together.

"It was a perfect place for an artist. It was downtown, it had parking, and the first weekend I was there; I had my son come visit me."

Visits expanded to shared custody and now Charles and son Chaly live close to downtown Los Angeles in a two-bedroom apartment filled with joy and with art. "I get up every morning at 5:30 am to iron his clothes, make his breakfast and drive him to school. He is my life."

His life includes work towards a Masters Degree in Art Therapy and a deepened relationship with his older children. His son Charles Cory and grandson CJ live in Washington D.C. His two daughters, Sydney and Jody, are in college in Northern California.

"I have made a full commitment to art. I am working to build a body of work. Except for raising my son, it is the most difficult endeavor of my life. Going back to school humbles you. I take solace in knowing I can help people with art.

"I am going to help people by showing them by example that a path out of nothingness is possible. If it happened for me, it can happen for you."

Charles Bivians

DEBORAH MARTIN

Creating Something Beautiful

"Creating something beautiful from scraps" is what Deborah Martin does every day. As a quilter, her work has been displayed in galleries and public buildings. As the Resident Property Manager of SRO Housing Corporation's Gateways Apartments, she has a hand in creating beautiful new beginnings for formerly homeless men and women. The Gateways Apartments, newly constructed affordable housing which opened in 2013, rises above the despair of the streets in the heart of Skid Row at the corner of 5th and San Pedro Streets.

Deborah has experienced homelessness first hand. Like many of the residents who live in SRO Housing Corporation's residential buildings in Skid Row, her journey back from homelessness was stitched together with tenacity, commitment and hope.

She was first hired by SRO Housing as a Janitor and worked her way up to on-site Property Manager entrusted with 108 units for chronically homeless men and women. She has also been responsible for the lease-up and management of several SRO Housing properties, including the Yankee Apartments (80 efficiency units), the New Terminal (40 efficiency units) and the Marshal House (71 units).

The Gateways Apartments is a contemporary six-story building that opens to the community with an airy courtyard and lush greenery. The building overlooks a neighborhood that serves as ground zero for the homeless in Los Angeles. The setting is about as far as one can get from the "Ozzie and Harriet, picket fence life" that Deborah lost when divorce and a drug habit propelled her into a life of drugs and prostitution nearly two decades ago.

> **"When I ended up on the streets, drugs helped to kill the pain. My whole world had shattered and the drugs kept me numb for a long time."**

Deborah lived on the streets or in motels for six years. She had worked in the MacArthur Park area before the divorce, and when she found herself homeless she went there. Her parents, siblings, even her ex-husband, searched the park for her. "I worried the death out of them. I'd see them and exit the other side. They loved me, but I didn't feel that I could go home."

During her years on the streets, Deborah was frequently arrested.

> **"Once you've been to jail, you keep going back. Drugs and prostitution kept leading me to jail, and eventually to prison. It was hard."**

After her release in September 2000, Deborah lived at the Weingart Center and found work through Chrysalis. She spent time on the Central City East Association's Street Works Team

DEBORAH MARTIN

and swept the curbs of Skid Row. Then, Deborah was hired at SRO Housing Corporation's Leonide Hotel as a Janitor where the manager wrote her a letter of recommendation. In 2002, she was hired by SRO Housing Corporation as a full-time Assistant Manager at the Courtland Apartments and she was on her way to establishing herself as an award-winning staff member.

In 2003, Deborah received the Chrysalis "Butterfly of the Year" Award. "That was really an honor. Chrysalis gave me my start. For someone like me, someone starting all over, cleaning up past wreckage, they were a lifesaver. Today, I send my residents who are looking for work to them."

Deborah is recognized as a gifted mentor who supervises and trains SRO Housing Corporation property management staff. She is grateful for the opportunities the organization has provided her in her job and as a person.

"SRO means a lot to me. I came to SRO Housing Corporation looking for a place I could grow, and I've found that. I'm not the same person I was so many years ago when I came to work here."

"The learning never stops. You learn how to deal with different people and situations in different ways. I take my job seriously. I'm not here just for the paycheck. My job is about giving back to the community that gave to me when I needed them. I know I'm only one hit away from being the curb one more time."

Despite personal tragedy, including the sudden death of one of her sons, and deaths of several close family members, Deborah remains committed to the new life she has built at SRO Housing Corporation. "Today I'm just not willing to give up what I've worked so hard to achieve."

"I'm not proud of what I did back then, but I don't think I'd be the person I am today if I hadn't gone through what I did. I'm far from perfect. I still have a lot of work to do on me."

In addition to her work as Resident Manager of SRO Housing Corporation at the Gateways Apartments, Deborah relaxes by creating beautiful quilts and is active in a Skid Row quilters' group that meets regularly in the community.

>"I've come a long way. My journey continues."
> Deborah Martin

SERVICE

"Helping others heal is good for me."

Daniel Castilleja

DANIEL CASTILLEJA

Helping Others Heal

Daniel Castilleja's ground-floor studio apartment is just steps away from the chaos and despair of Skid Row just outside his window. His tidy home at the James Wood Apartments is an oasis of serenity, decorated with art and displays of Daniel's handmade silk flower creations.

"This is my first apartment ever!" marvels Daniel, who became homeless after an injury forced him to leave his live-in care-giving job, "I didn't know what to do." He lived in his car and for a time slept in the stairwell of an apartment building.

A caregiver for over 21 years, Daniel was cared for as a child by six older sisters and an array of aunts. He had never known his mother, who disappeared after his parents' divorce when he was very young. In his twenties, he searched for and found her and established a relationship despite his sisters' disapproval. "My mom had become an alcoholic and had been diagnosed with schizophrenia. She did not take medication. We became friends and I am glad that I got to know her before she passed away. Now my sisters wish they had done that too."

His sisters, all high achievers, graduated at the top of their classes and built families and powerful professional careers. That wasn't possible for Daniel who learned only later in life that his academic struggles were due to dyslexia, "I went to college but I did not finish. I was tired.

"I felt stupid. I felt like such a failure." When he lost his job, Daniel tried stealing food to survive, but success eluded him in that as well, "They caught me the first time."

"I went to jail. I was very ashamed. The worst thing was that my father was disappointed in me."

Then, Daniel found his way to Skid Row. "I had never been downtown. I went the Union Rescue Mission and then to the Russ Hotel," says Daniel.

The Russ Hotel provides Emergency Housing in safe, clean, private rooms for homeless persons coming directly from the streets.

"I was strong because of my dad." His father, who lives in Texas, plays an important role in Daniel's life. "I talk to him two or three times a week. Saying 'I love you' has always been difficult for him. One day, even though I had disappointed him, he recognized how hard I was trying and he told me, 'I think you're the smartest of the whole group.' he said, 'You solve your own problems. You're smart.' That was so important for me."

DANIEL CASTILLEJA

Daniel is clearly moved as he recalls the distance he has traveled since coming to Skid Row and SRO Housing Corporation.

> **"I have always been in care-giving. When I needed help, SRO saved me."**

All the resources I got here, it is overwhelming for me. I want to pay back. I have goals now, to finish school and to go into social work. I want to get off government assistance and move to another apartment. I want to move on to let someone else experience this beautiful apartment. I want to be a positive influence."

Daniel is an active SRO Housing volunteer at community events and welcomes visitors to his home as a stop on SRO Housing tours of Skid Row.

> **"SRO Housing gave me an apartment. I am very grateful. I appreciate my home so much."**

Daniel keeps busy. He creates silk floral arrangements from scavenged materials and gives them away as gifts to his neighbors. He has discovered a gift for writing and has had several essays published in the National Association of Case Management (NACM) newsletter. He wrote a winning nomination for his SRO Case Manager, Juan Carlos Callejas, who was presented with the XCEL Award at the 2013 NACM conference. He has also been recognized for excellence as a volunteer. This belated accomplishment has inspired Daniel to do more for others. "If I only knew earlier that I was dyslexic, my childhood pain would have been so different. Now, I'm doing well. SRO has been a part of that."

IT ALL BEGINS WITH A HOME

To give back, Daniel spends time on the streets of Skid Row.

"People don't choose to be homeless. I go up to people and I say hello. I don't care if they are dirty or stinky. I want to let people know I've been in their shoes. My heart is healing. I feel loved and appreciated. Helping others heal is good for me."

Daniel Castellija

EDUARDO "EDDIE" PEREZ

I Reached My Goal

Eddie Perez describes himself well.

> **"I come with a laugh on my face."**

    Cheerful, even effervescent, Eddie is SRO Housing Corporation's Facilities Management Maintenance Foreman and he is one of our longest-serving employees, hired in April 1986.

    Eddie has seen the organization, and the community, change dramatically over the years. "When I first came here, it was bad, real bad. Now, Anita Nelson (SRO Housing Corporation CEO) is doing good things," says Eddie. When he was first hired, the organization had developed only one building. Since then, 30 residential buildings and other projects have been completed. "The tenants live better now. When I first came here, the rooms only had a sink. Now, they have kitchens and they have bigger rooms. I am proud of the corporation," says Eddie.

His facilities maintenance team completes up to 70 work orders per month for repairs, renovations and refurbishments of worn and damaged apartment units and equipment. Eddie's knack for fixing things is built upon his early experience in the Hughes Aircraft machine shop and spills over to his relationships in the community. "I see peoples' physiognomy. Sometimes they are depressed. They tell me to come back another day. I come back the next day and maybe they are feeling better. Sometimes they over-medicate. Some are still on drugs. If they are hungry, I never give them money. I go and buy some food."

Eddie has found a balance between his work and his home life. "When I get on the freeway to go home, I leave my work behind." His wife of nearly 30 years is a Kindergarten teacher and their three grown daughters are building futures for themselves...with Eddie's help.

"I reached my goal. I sent all three of my daughters to college," says Eddie, with a broad smile. One daughter has graduated with an engineering degree, one is in medical school, and another is completing a business administration degree.

> **"I am not a rich person. That is the best thing I can do for my kids, send them to school. Life has been good to me. I have a job that I like for 28 years. I like what I am doing. I am helping others. That is what my father and mother told me. I am happy to do that."**
>
> **Eddie Perez**

RON SMITH

Focused on Helping

Ron Smith has a degree in communications and was a news cameraperson before relocating to Los Angeles. He is the Resident Manager of our SRO Housing Corporation Ellis Hotel, with 56 units for at-risk elderly including those with special needs. He is also a member of the Downtown Los Angeles Neighborhood Council (DLANC) and a videographer with an abiding passion for our community.

Ron epitomizes our SRO Housing Corporation commitment to community engagement and partnerships, "I'm involved in several community organizations that work to make Skid Row a better place to live including DLANC, Pepperdine University, New City Church of Downtown Los Angeles and others. All of these organizations have adopted the Ellis Hotel and our residents. They help by providing house cleaning, hygiene kits, socks, and other everyday items the residents need."

IT ALL BEGINS WITH A HOME

"In the past I assisted organizations with set-up at Gladys Park and have even sponsored events there through the Affordable Housing Committee and the Parks Recreation and Open Spaces Committee of DLANC. One of the organizations I've assisted, Operation Help the Homeless (OHTH) recently used our dining room as a staging area as they set up to deliver more than 500 blankets to people sleeping on the streets," says Ron.

"As a way of saying thank you for our help, they donated turkeys and trimmings for our Thanksgiving Dinner here at the Ellis. Volunteers from the building cooked and distributed food to the residents and the group enjoyed it so much they decided to come back again in December."

The holidays are a particularly difficult time for our residents, many of whom are disengaged from family. "We become their family," says Anita Nelson, CEO of SRO Housing Corporation.

Residents of the Ellis are low-income seniors. Ron knows and cares about each of the residents.

"Some have previously been homeless. Some are low-income retirees. And many are alone in the world.

All of them enjoyed the holiday celebration. It was served by volunteers. We even had music from a guy in the building who plays at all the neighborhood parties. He brought his keyboard and played for us."

Ron came to SRO Housing Corporation through his work with Pepperdine University Palmer Center Entrepreneur-in-Training

RON SMITH

Program for disadvantaged people. He was tasked with recruiting residents of Skid Row who were bused to Pepperdine's Malibu campus for a class in entrepreneurship. Graduates of the 26-week program then received help in starting their own businesses. Ron worked as a coordinator for Micro Enterprise, "a model that works very well in the developing world. With different dynamics, it has already had a lot of success in Skid Row. There is a guy who opened a recycling business around the corner from the Ellis Hotel, on Stanford Street. He turned the hustle of recycling into a legitimate business."

Ron glows with excitement as he describes other examples of successful businesses resulting from the program including a transportation company that transports families to visit prisons, a mobile car wash, even a licensed T-shirt dealer authorized to sell at sports facilities.

> **"There are lots of opportunities here on Skid Row and I am focused on helping make them work."**
> **Ron Smith**

STARTING OVER

"Just because you have a disability or misfortune in life, doesn't mean that you have to forfeit your dreams and goals."

Jonathan Davis

JONATHAN DAVIS

Tragedy into Action

Hurricane Katrina survivor Jonathan Davis is a whirlwind. An activist and advocate, Jonathan has a ready smile and a passion for achievement. His multifaceted resume includes an ongoing role overseeing civic engagement and volunteers with the offices of Los Angeles Mayor Eric Garcetti. Jonathan has transformed his displacement from hurricane-ravaged New Orleans to action on behalf of others whose lives were altered by the storm, connecting them to resources and opportunities. He has transformed his diagnosis of Bipolar Disorder complicated by PTSD to positive action on behalf of others living with life-altering disabilities by becoming a trained facilitator, Peer Advocate and Program Navigator.

"Just because you have a disability or misfortune in life, doesn't mean that you have to forfeit your dreams and goals."

IT ALL BEGINS WITH A HOME

Ten years ago, Jonathan was a life-skills teacher for high-school age students with physical and mental disabilities in New Orleans. The school was destroyed in the storm. Several students and community members who had taken shelter there were killed. Jonathan and his family, including a disabled sister, sheltered in place in their home and experienced the terrifying storm at their doorstep. They were evacuated to the Super Dome in Houston, Texas, where Jonathan and his sister briefly became separated, and were soon offered shelter in 49 states.

"I was distraught. I was devastated. We could go anyplace but home to start over."

Jonathan landed in Los Angeles and quickly set about rebuilding his life. "I went to the Department of Rehabilitation and Employment Services and I typed up a resume. I got a job, and then I got a better job. I began processing things with drugs and alcohol. I had been running from the things I needed to deal with, the trauma of the storm, the loss of my home and my hometown."

Dedicated to a dream of becoming an entrepreneur, Jonathan strategically decided on Skid Row as a place where he could dedicate his formidable energy to healing and recovery.

"I needed a roof over my head, food in my belly, and clothes on my back. Thanks to SRO Housing, I am able to grow slowly and surely."

JONATHAN DAVIS

I am able to keep better control of past behaviors, drugs, depression, self doubt and I am learning to deal with my diagnosis."

He is also sharing his insight with others, connecting people to resources, employment opportunities, and helps them get to a place where they can move forward.

Jonathan believes strongly in living his truth.

"As an openly gay African American man, I have been accosted, and yet I have not been defeated. I have not held my head down. I am afraid that people do not see the greatness in themselves. I feel that I am effective in reaching people on Skid Row because I have been there, I got through it. I have insight to help others get to a place where they can move forward."

Jonathan Davis

OCTAVIA HAMLETT

No Longer a Professional Victim

Octavia Hamlett has transformed herself and her life since moving to Los Angeles from Las Vegas in 2011. "I was doing sex work in Las Vegas. Prostitution is addictive. You get addicted to the money. I got here to Los Angeles and gave it up and started the uncomfortable journey of not having money."

She stayed in Hollywood on a friend's couch and began to rethink her life.

"I had a fear-based outlook on life. I was a professional victim. I could not understand why I kept going in circles and circles."

She found her way to Skid Row and sought shelter at a mission. "I was terrified. It was wall to wall people. I saw people shooting up in the daytime. These were people who live in pain. There was pain, anger, aggression on the street. I was not used to it. It was overwhelming."

Octavia is a transgender woman of color, dark skinned, stunningly attractive with a magnetic smile and a clear sense of self that has evolved in recent years. "It has been an amazing journey. I realize I am in the midst of angels on Skid Row. I have given my life to Christ. That got me on the road and got me to embrace who I was supposed to be...within my relationship to clients and within my LGBT community.

"I empower transgender women who don't feel they are enough."

By helping other transgender women, Octavia has taken on a leadership role. She shares her story to serve as a role model and credits her faith for her ability to help others

"I share with women who can't see their own beauty. I share with the prostitute who thinks she can't do anything. I share about feeling as if you are dirt. I share that I was once the victim of my childhood.

I healed from those wounds. I tell my story in hopes that younger people will not take so long to heal. I had family issues and addiction issues."

She places a hand gently over her heart, "The truth is in here. I am a truth-teller.

It took living on Skid Row to get tougher. You can't break me. I remember where I came from.

"I embrace the fact that I was born male. I know who I am. I have learned to love myself."

She has also learned to trust her natural boldness as a gift. She entered a beauty pageant and despite her initial reluctance, she won.

"I put on my sneakers and wore my crown back to Skid Row. It proved to me that I am more than I think I am."

"Now, I know I can change this world. It is my duty and my honor to help others feel good about themselves, especially when the world tries to tell them they are not enough."

Octavia Hamlett

MELINDA BOLTON

Tired of Living Out of Bags

Melinda had been homeless for four years. "I stayed with friends, but they put you out when you run out of money. It has been hard...."

> **"Living in the streets, living in cars, nothing to eat. It's hard when you get sick, when you have nowhere to go. It makes you feel worthless."**

Petite and stoic, Melinda's guarded dignity suggests a dramatic journey. She is reluctant to share details and yet what she leaves unsaid touches on past struggles.

> **"I've been through hell and back and I don't want to rely on anybody but myself. I've slept in cars. I've slept on the street. I've had nothing."**

IT ALL BEGINS WITH A HOME

She brightens when she considers the advantages of her new home at the Gateways Apartments.

"I won't have to live out of bags. I'll hang up my clothes. I'll have my own bed, my own shower. It will be marvelous!"

Her smile is interrupted with a twinge of anticipatory anxiety, and a flurry of questions.

"Will I need to buy a blanket? Will I need pots and pans? When will I be able to move in? Will I be able to have guests?"

Guests are important to Melinda as she has plans for her future.

"I want to cook. I'll make smothered pork chops and vegetables. I want to get married again. I want to achieve something in life."

Melinda Bolton

BRENDA WITTEN

With a roof over my head...

Soon after settling into a tent she shared near 7th Street, Brenda found a lump in her breast.

She lost her parents, members of extended family and her husband to cancer, so her fears for her health prognosis are rooted in painful memories, "I watched them die," she says as her hazel eyes well with tears,

> **"I know I have a higher chance of getting cancer, I have an appointment scheduled and I am afraid."**

Brenda was raised on a farm and had learned to drive a tractor by the time she was five years old. After her husband died, she was drawn into battle with severe depression that has shadowed her for

IT ALL BEGINS WITH A HOME

years as she has moved in and out of homelessness. "I've bounced around," she says as she sums up her life journey.

Brenda had been homeless since 2006 when an altercation with her landlord led to a psychiatric hospitalization and a release that left her on Skid Row with medication and temporary housing. For a time, she lived at SRO Housing Golden West Hotel. Then, a move to live with a friend fizzled when his drinking put her back on the streets. She found her way to Texas, where her children and grandchildren live. Difficulties arose in getting her medications refilled and accessing mental health care in a rural community lacking public transportation. She soon realized that Skid Row offered the services she needed and returned to Los Angeles.

Even with a potential cancer diagnosis, Brenda remains upbeat. She is one of 500 chronically homeless men and women who applied for an apartment and one of the 108 who were selected for new homes at the Gateways Apartments., "I have a service dog, so I won't be alone, but this will be the first place I've ever had to myself. I like having a place where I don't have to wait to use the toilet."

She has moved into her new apartment at SRO Housing Corporation's Gateways Apartments with her dog, Reeses, and is enjoying her new home. Fortunately, the lump has proven not to be cancerous and follow-up treatment has begun.

"With a roof over my head, I'll be able to focus on getting well."
Brenda Witten

ANTHONY VILLARREAL

My Own Paris

Fashion designer, Anthony Villarreal, lives in SRO Housing's Rivers Artist Lofts.

His live/work loft space is colorful and carefully balanced between cutting and sewing space, décor and display space, creative living space and a lovingly tended green space/garden patio facing the back parking lot.

"I am proud that I stayed true to my vision. Much of what I design is asymmetrical. I explore within my aesthetic for transformational ways to create. Today, a designer must make clothes for real people." His fashion line Agave Couture was inspired by his sisters' ample curves and informed by his years in Paris. His elegant

designs flatter every woman and feature soft, floating fabrics and his signature lantern sleeve.

Anthony grew up during the Chicano student movement in Southern California in the 1970's and was empowered and proud of his roots. "My journey took me through various modes of design and propelled me to jump out of my comfort zone and dare to live in a foreign country."

He won a design contest which afforded a trip to Paris to attend the Paris Fashion Institute for one month. He decided to stay and his journey began to unfold.

"I moved to Paris as a young man and learned about creative camaraderie through the expat community. Everything was new and different."

"Paris is the Haute Couture capital...but times are changing and creative influences are world-wide. I began to feel I was losing my identity. My cultural identity has always been a part of my design identity. I became desperate to re-connect with my family. There was also a volatile feeling of anti-Americanism in the air."

After 20 years in Paris, Anthony decided to return to the United States.

"When I returned, I was staying with family in Southern California but had no home in Los Angeles. I needed a place to nurture my creative work."

"A friend encouraged me to complete an application for this space. I was one of six artists selected."

ANTHONY VILLARREAL

"This is like a dream. I am able to do what I love in a live-work space. I have created my own Paris here in Los Angeles."

Anthony Villarreal

PATRICIA LIPKINS

The Happiest Person

Patricia is a resident of the Gateways Apartments. Her story was featured on the United Way Home for Good website:

"In 2013, Patricia received the keys to her new home. She is housed in SRO Housing's Gateways Apartments. Patricia was matched to one of the 80 vacancies in the new Gateways Apartments. After 11 years of homelessness, Patricia was overcome with emotion as she accepted the keys to her new apartment."

Patricia was raised in Foster Care in Ohio after her birth parents abandoned their five children in an apartment building.

IT ALL BEGINS WITH A HOME

"My mom decided she didn't want to be a mother anymore. I was one year old."

Her mother surfaced when Patricia was a teenager and invited Patricia to visit her in Los Angeles. Determined to reconnect with her mother, she traveled by bus with only the clothes on her back. It did not work out the way she imagined it would. "We fought and mom kicked me out. I started walking the streets."

She also started using drugs, even while attending school to train to be a nurse. "Even though I got high, I still got 100% on my class work." After several starts and stops, she completed her training and worked in health care facilities and as a private duty nurse until a back injury sidelined her career. A brief marriage also had an impact. Her husband, a devout Muslim, drove her to escape to Skid Row. "He was everywhere. I didn't feel comfortable. I ended up downtown. I was still smoking. I smoked crack cocaine for 13 years here in Skid Row. I knew what I was doing was wrong. I went to the mission and I told them I wanted to quit."

To enter a treatment program she had to be tested for HIV. It was 1993 and she tested positive.

"I cried for a whole week. I cursed God." Since then, she has achieved sobriety, moved into her new home and has cultivated a deepening relationship with her mother and siblings. A family reunion is on the horizon.

"Today I have a different mindset. I shine a light in me. I am the happiest person"

She keeps busy, planning community meals and activities at the Gateways Apartments.

PATRICIA LIPKINS

"We have movie nights. I provide everything; popcorn, jujubes…it makes me feel joy."

Patricia Lipkins

DENISE DRINKARD PHILLIPS

Going to be Awesome

Denise Phillips falters as she remembers watching her beloved cat, Big Head, bask in the sunlight that last time before she drove away to sell her car.

"He loved that spot. He didn't know I wasn't coming back.

I drove away and I watched him in the mirror..."

She catches her breath, lowers her eyes, as if seeing that sunny spot once again.

After a long pause, she sighs, "I know the neighbors are taking care of him. I sneaked over there to visit, and he wanted to follow me back. But I can't, you know. I love that cat...but I can't."

Denise lost everything when her husband's death led to the loss of their home. She gradually sold off possessions, letting go of cherished memories to pay bills, and feed herself and her cat. "It got harder," she says as she catalogues a series of difficulties that drove her to homelessness. There were too many bills to pay. She could not manage the house, the car; the loneliness ... even caring for the cat became overwhelming. She started using drugs.

> **"I was on a Board of Directors. I had a vote. I was an Intake Counselor and I taught a Domestic Violence class. I helped people. Then, I disappeared. I went to lunch one day and I never went back."**

She headed to downtown Los Angeles' Skid Row where 5th Street is known as 'The Nickel' and where tents, sidewalk homeless encampments and drug use are commonplace. "Back in the 1940's there used to be homes there. Kids used to play in the streets." Not now. The streets of Skid Row are known to draw those under the spell of addiction, and those who prey upon them.

> **"You can get lost on the nickel. You put up a tent and no one knows you're there."**

Denise managed to find her way out of her addiction, and is now struggling to rebuild her support system, "I'm not hard to find. When he can, my baby brother comes to see me. But the rest of my family is gone. It hurts that my older brother hasn't shown up for me. I asked God, 'Why are you taking all these people out of my life?' I haven't heard from my family in New Orleans since Hurricane Katrina. My husband is dead, my parents are deceased and I haven't seen my sister in 15 years. I don't know what I've done to drive her away. Or I don't remember. And my husband's family doesn't even know he's dead. I'm tired, and I'm scared, and I'm lonely. I've been through so much."

As she prepares to start over, Denise is recovering from surgery in a convalescent home and hoping for a slot on the SRO Housing Waiting List. She gestures to her hospital gown, the worn surroundings, "This is not me. I liked to be dressed up, to have my nails done." She is determined to reshape her life. "You'll see, once I have a place to stay and somewhere to lay my head…

"I am going to be awesome!"
Denise Phillips

LEYMOINE BOLTON

Look a Certain Way

"Sartorial splendor" is not a phrase that comes to mind when one thinks of residents of Skid Row and yet Leymoine Bolton is a man who knows his way around a wardrobe. When he attended the grand opening of our Gateways Apartments, he was "suited and booted for the occasion," and his day-to-day duds are decidedly high-end.

"All my things went into storage, and I have nice things. Now that I have a home, I can enjoy my clothes again. I like to dress well."

And yet as a well-dressed man, Leymoine does stand out on Skid Row,

IT ALL BEGINS WITH A HOME

"People tell me 'Why are you down here? You don't look like you need to be here. But you don't have to look a certain way to need help."

Leymoine's journey began when his father passed away and family members began a bitter fight over the family home and money. He left the turmoil behind and ended up living in his car, camping out in a McDonald's parking lot at night and volunteering as an HIV/AIDS advocate during the day. He was diagnosed with HIV in 1995 and fell ill with AIDS in 1999.

"I was sick. I had one foot in the grave and I was ready to walk in with the other."

After his recovery, Leymoine became increasingly active as an advocate for prevention of HIV/AIDS, "Now, I tell people to use a condom, get to a clinic, get checked out."

His work as an advocate blossomed into a leadership role on the board of a clinic in South Los Angeles, To Help Everyone (T.H.E.) Clinic. He has testified on behalf of the clinic before the United States Congress, speaking to the need for uninterrupted funding for Federally Qualified Health Centers. "Budget cuts would be devastating to the community and to patients."

When Leymoine first came to the clinic in 2009, "I was just a patient. Then, they asked me to speak. Now, I am the Secretary of the Board of Directors on the Executive Committee."

Leymoine lives at SRO Housing Golden West Hotel where the majority of his neighbors live with a mental illness. "We share a bathroom, one on each floor, and there is a shared kitchen. Some of the residents are still using drugs. I can't control their lives. I can only tell them to 'slow the roll."

LEYMOINE BOLTON

"Overall, we look out for one another. The services are available here," says Leymoine.

"I came here because all my resources had dried up. My family was not a place I could go for help. I had to make it on my own. I was ashamed at first, but now I am at peace. I have a place now to rest and rebuild."

Leymoine Bolton

DEIDRE MAYES

It's Temporary

Deidre's smile is even brighter in person. The blurred photo of her smiling after winning our SRO Housing annual Domino's Tournament focuses on her smile. It is hard to imagine that smile has been touched by tragedy.

Deidre grew up in Los Angeles where her grandfather taught her to play Dominos. "Every day after school I'd go to my Nana's house and Grandpa would challenge me to a game of Dominos. He taught me by beating me. He wasn't easy on me. I just kept coming back and I kept getting better." When SRO Housing socialization activities announced a Dominos Tournament, she was eager to play, "I thought, bring it on!" She won every game in her building and then moved up to win every game against champions from other SRO Housing residences.

She relishes the memory, "I'm the Champ!" She is upbeat about her life and accomplishments, particularly her two daughters. "They are the best things I ever did. I have no regrets. They are twenty years apart in age. My youngest, she was a 'whoops' but I am so glad to have her in my life. They are very different. My oldest, she is a social butterfly and my youngest is a planner."

A career paralegal, Deidre had settled in the high desert community of Victorville in Northern Los Angeles County. She was planning to open a beauty salon to carry her through retirement. She had graduated from beauty school and obtained her license when her brother called her from South Los Angeles and convinced her to join him in a new business venture.

Her brother was also a trained paralegal and was preparing to open a bankruptcy business with an investor. He needed his sister's trusted skills and she gave up her home in the desert to move in with her brother to help him achieve his dream.

In one devastating moment, everything changed. They were driving through Central Los Angeles when he became ensnarled in an argument with the driver of another car. Her brother and the other driver exchanged words and jockeyed for position on the street. When they came to a stoplight, a tractor-trailer truck pulled between the two cars, unaware of the escalating tensions between the two drivers. Her brother, bothered by the obstruction of the truck, stepped out of the car to lean beneath the truck to continue his harangue of the other driver. Deidre watched helplessly as the light changed, the truck moved forward, and her brother was crushed beneath the weight of the double-axle rear wheels.

Her brother's dream of starting a business died with him. Deidre planned his funeral while packing up to move out of his apartment.

DEIDRE MAYES

She had nowhere to go and was haunted by traumatic memories of the grisly scene of her brother's death. "It was like a movie. You see it coming but there's nothing you can do about it. The light changes. The wheels roll forward. There's no stopping it." She needed help.

She began seeing Dr. McCarthy at the Downtown Mental Health Center and credits the help she received there for leading her to access Emergency Housing at the Russ Hotel. Later, she was able to move to a beautiful new apartment at the renovated Ford Apartments.

"It is lovely. I have my place fixed up real nice. But don't try going outside at night. This neighborhood is dirty and grungy. I'm getting older and I want to have a nicer neighborhood to live in." Deidre has a plan, "I pay my rent right on time every month so I can build up a good renter's record. Then, when I find some other place to move, they'll see I'm a good resident and they'll help me."

"This is a nice place, but it is not the neighborhood I want to be in. For me, it's temporary. It's like being broke. I do not have a lot of money. It's true that I'm broke, but that is only temporary.

"Being poor is a state of being, but being broke…that can change!"
Deidre Mayes

TG

Hungry for Better Life

TG is younger than most Avenues to Work program participants, only twenty-five years old. He is already a father, a veteran of homelessness and of youthful "running in the streets." He has a simple goal,

> **"I am trying to live for the rest of my life."**

With a chilling simplicity TG describes his own funeral, "I want to leave a legacy. When people talk at my funeral I want them to say I was a father, a brother, a hard working man." He is haunted by time wasted in his youth.

IT ALL BEGINS WITH A HOME

"I took the wrong path earlier in my life. I wish I had stopped earlier. I made mistakes. Now, I just want to see my son grow up to be a man. I want to see him have kids of his own. I want to survive for him."

With a home, a job and a future, TG may very well have that opportunity. Avenues to Work provided TG with housing and meals while he looked for a job and developed the habit of waking up early to check job leads. "The jobs are out there. It depends on you. If you want it bad enough, the jobs are there for you." TG's job search efforts paid off, "I sent my resume, I got called in for an interview and I got hired to work the next day."

While in the Avenues to Work Program, meals and housing were provided free of charge. "They even provided transportation to job interviews. They made it easy." TG's goal of achieving independence was of primary importance. He had experienced homelessness by 'sofa surfing,' churning through the grudging hospitality of friends and family long enough to awaken an appetite for his own home.

"I had three months of housing in the Avenues to Work Program and I saved my money while I was in the program. I have an apartment now. I did it."

TG has a short walk to work in the bustling downtown Los Angeles clothing industry and has ambitions beyond his current job.

He dreams of starting his own business.

"I'm hungry for a better life. In the future, twenty, forty, sixty years from now, I want to be in my own office. I would like to make it to 105. That would be great, just to breathe at one hundred and five years old. I'm working on it."

TG

VETERANS

*"Some people see it as a success,
I see it as possible."*

Chris Zamor

DAVID

The Best thing that Ever Happened

David, a veteran of the Air Force, doesn't dwell on his military service, preferring to focus on regaining his high-flying success in the entertainment business.

> **"I was a millionaire. I was a successful businessman. Drug dependence changed that. I started smoking a lot of weed, and I just gave it all up."**

When he dropped out of sight, David's contemporaries assumed he was on sabbatical. Instead, David spent the time homeless and in jail.

IT ALL BEGINS WITH A HOME

"My bottom was when I was in LA County jail. In fact, being in jail and being on Skid Row was the best thing that ever happened to me."

David was forced to look at his life and was inspired to make meaningful changes.

"I thought, 'How am I going to dig my way out of here?' I decided to do whatever it takes."

"Now, my career is the best it has ever been," says David, (who recently re-married) referring to the turn his life has taken since he found his way to SRO Housing Corporation's Veterans' Transitional Program. He was referred to the program by Veteran's Affairs (VA) after being released from jail. David participated in the program, took part in groups, followed the rules, and worked to expand his skill-sets.

While in the program, he got sober, stopped smoking, and started running regularly. His asthma is now in remission, "my health is better than ever," and his career is back on track. He also credits the program with giving him an opportunity to try his wings, allowing forays into off-site consulting while still in the program and making it possible for him to save seed money for a new start. He ultimately relocated outside of California where consulting jobs have led to lucrative new ventures. He has reconnected with a previous business partner to re-establish his reputation, and rebuild his resume.

"Life," David says, "is so good."

"Getting out of Skid Row was the biggest challenge of my life. I am haunted by the knowledge that a lot of people don't make it out."

DAVID

David is mindful of the role SRO Housing Corporation Veteran's Transitional Program played. "The organization helped save my life. I am so grateful." He has special praise for program staff Jeffrey Proctor, Veteran's Transitional Program Coordinator: "I think the world of Jeff. He made a real difference. He treated me with dignity. He treated me with respect"

"I am so thankful to SRO Housing and the Veterans' Program, I am so grateful."

WILLIAM CARR

I Never Thought I Would be This Old

William Carr is quick to tell you that he's a liar.

> "I warn you, I lie a lot. And I'm always joking. But this is the true part…"

    A native of Brooklyn, New York, William volunteered for the Air Corps in 1941 and served in England in World War II. His brother, a pilot, was shot down and spent time as a prisoner of war. "I haven't spoken to him in years. I'm not sure if he is still alive or not."

    William is elfin, short of stature and tall of tales. He traveled from the East Coast to California with stops in Chicago and in Las Vegas along the way. He was drawn to Las Vegas by his love of gambling and to Los Angeles by his love of 'the ponies." He spends his happiest hours at the racetrack, diligently budgeting

IT ALL BEGINS WITH A HOME

for his gambling each month. He made a decision in his youth to avoid marriage in favor of gambling. "Sometimes you're up when you're winning. Sometimes you're down. Kids gotta eat; rent's gotta be paid. When you're a gambler you can't be counted on, so I just decided to avoid all that."

He has lived in the Skid Row community since 1954 and has lived in several SRO Housing properties, even before they were purchased and renovated by the organization. He lived at the Ford Hotel and at the Russ Hotel before moving to his current home in the Courtland Apartments nearly two decades ago. It was there that he celebrated his 92nd birthday in November 2013.

(PHOTO) William Carr with photos of his first car and of himself and family before leaving for service in WWII.

"I tell you what, I never thought I would be this old, but I never think of dying.

I watch sports all day long, every day, unless I'm at the track. It's pretty simple. It's a good life."

He shows off carefully preserved photos of himself smiling in a shiny new Packard convertible and standing proudly next to family members in his military uniform. His brother was the first to enlist in the military, just before the outbreak of WWII, and William followed his example soon after.

WILLIAM CARR

William has been out of touch with his family for years yet takes comfort in the Skid Row community he calls home.

William has high praise for the Courtland Apartments, "The staff is great. I have my meals delivered by Meals on Wheels and I have the bathroom down the hall. It's clean and it's affordable. Not like on the Westside, where the rents are so high."

His room is tidy and simply decorated with a prized Veterans' Day commendation from the City of Los Angeles taped to the wall. There are newspapers, folded to the sports pages,stacked neatly on a small dresser and a desktop TV is silently tuned to the sports channel.

> **"I have everything I need."**
> **William Carr**

CHRIS ZAMOR

Homeless and Got a Masters Degree

While Chris Zamor completed his undergraduate degree at UCLA and later, during his graduate work at USC, he commuted to campus from Skid Row.

> **"It was surreal. While residing at SRO Housing, I managed to complete a degree at UCLA and then, in the Veteran's Transitional Program in 2012, I completed my Master's Degree in teaching at USC."**

Originally from New Jersey, Chris's desire to be a history teacher helped him face urban inner city challenges of drugs, violence, and a fractured family. He joined the military after high school but "my Navy career did not turn out as I planned because of bad decisions with my anger. It will always be a regret that I did not see that through." His education, too, did not turn out as planned. While an undergraduate at UCLA, he was charged with a serious offense and was incarcerated, "There was no hope. I had a severe anger issue. My family wasn't with me." Later, he ended up on Skid Row.

"I was freezing, out in the elements, no one to turn to. That's hard."

Chris learned about SRO Housing Corporation through word of mouth. "In the military, you have a lifelong fraternity that transcends race, age, everything. Veterans are a resource. "I learned about SRO and thankfully, I got into Emergency Housing at the Russ Hotel and the Veteran's Transitional Program." It was a relief.

"The biggest thing with homelessness is not having a sense of security, no sense of comfort. I couldn't settle down, I couldn't bathe, I couldn't be clean."

In the Veterans Transitional Program, Chris could settle down and take on the hard work of transformation. The Veterans Transitional Program provides housing and case management free of charge to Veterans while they are in the program, allowing Veterans like Chris to save enough money to put a deposit down on an apartment. Participants invest hard work and perseverance. He is proud of his transition from homelessness and hopelessness.

CHRIS ZAMOR

"I weathered the storm. The sense of hopelessness is gone."
"Hey, I was homeless and now I have a Masters Degree.
Some people see it as a success story; I see it as possible."

Chris Zamor

DAVID ABEYTA

A Father for an Hour

David Abeyta lost everything. His marriage collapsed, his only child died, his health was in crisis and his mental health was tenuous. Then, he started gambling.

After serving in the military, David established a career in a Las Vegas casino, "I know," he laughs, "I was inside the gambling business. It's like making sausages, when you know what goes in to it, you know to stay away. I knew so much about it, I thought I could never get caught up in it." And yet the pull was overwhelming.

> **"Gambling allows you to be in a group and isolate at the same time. The lights and the people allow you to mask your depression. Of all the addictions, gambling addiction has the highest suicide rate."**

IT ALL BEGINS WITH A HOME

David was no exception. He survived a suicide attempt and realized he needed to explore the forces that drove his divorce. His wife was Pilipino and he felt that beyond the grief over the loss of their child, their cultural differences contributed to the breakup. He took a leave of absence, rented a beachfront cottage on the Philippine island of Cebu and tried to escape into the silence and simplicity of life.

"I woke up one morning and there was some rice on the stove that had spoiled." He was preparing to throw it away when his housekeeper, a local woman, stopped him. "She took the rice and spread it on a straw mat in the sunlight. After a few hours, it was as dry and as good as new. She was a simple woman with no education and she taught me a deep lesson. It seemed so logical to throw something away that appeared rotten. She showed me that it could be fixed. It opened a new window for me."

"I realized I wanted to live, and I didn't know how."

He returned to the states where more life lessons were in store. He journeyed through the loss of his career to his gambling addiction, the loss of his home, and grueling treatment for Hepatitis C contracted during his military service in the Air Force. The treatments brought him to Los Angeles where he is now starting a new life. David commutes from the Gateways Apartments to attend school with funds secured through the Veterans Re-Training Assistance Program. He is preparing to graduate with a Certificate in Drug and Alcohol Counseling. He also interns several hours a week, tutoring and counseling young addicts.

"It allows me to be a father for an hour or two every day."

DAVID ABEYTA

David' eyes mist behind stylish eyeglasses. He tosses aside his carefree manner and takes a pause to reflect on his new life at the Gateways Apartments.

"It is more than a building. It is home."

"SRO Housing saved my life. I was tired and I didn't have the strength. Trying to control my depression was like fighting a ghost. I was at the Russ Hotel and I had to have surgery. They saved my bed for me.

"It saved me in so many ways...just to know that somebody cared. Jeff, in the Veterans Transitional Program, and Dora, my Case Manager, I would not be here if it were not for them. Simple things mattered so much, like going on a picnic. They reminded me what it was like to be a member of a bonded group, like a family."

"I didn't get to see my child walk. I didn't get to help her grow up. But now, I am giving back and helping others.

"Through my work, I get to be the father I wanted to be. That brings me great peace. I'm grateful."

David Abeyta

A BRIEF HISTORY

James M. Wood, a visionary leader who served as the Chairman of the Community Redevelopment Agency of the City of Los Angeles, founded SRO Housing Corporation as a bold move to revitalize the Central City East community of downtown Los Angeles known as "Skid Row." We were granted independent non-profit status on February 14, 1984. Since that time, our impact and innovation have set us apart as one of the leading providers of affordable housing for homeless and low-income individuals in Los Angeles.

SRO Housing Corporation has a history of transforming dilapidated properties in downtown Los Angeles into comfortable, clean private rooms and beautiful contemporary studio apartments. Everything we do is focused on revitalizing the community. To date, we have developed over 2,300 units of housing and are recognized as one of the largest housing providers in the community. We are especially proud of our role in transforming people's lives through housing.

IT ALL BEGINS WITH A HOME

SRO Housing Corporation has had an important impact. Our renovation and development projects have included the transformation of the burned-out shell of the Yankee Cocktail Lounge into the Yankee Apartments and the resurrection of the infamous "Hotel Hell" as the new Ford Apartments.

In 2015, SRO Housing Corporation will celebrate the culmination of our 30th anniversary year with the opening of our 30th residential project, the Rosslyn Hotel Apartments.

ABOUT THE ORGANIZATION

How You Can Help

You can make it possible for SRO Housing Corporation to be there when there is no one else to turn to.

SRO Housing Corporation is a non-profit 501(c)(3) non-profit organization dedicated to building a vibrant community for homeless and very low-income individuals in the Skid Row area of downtown Los Angeles by providing clean, safe, and affordable housing; managing public spaces; and administering needed supportive services.

You can support this important work with a donation. Your contribution is tax deductible as allowed by law and is deeply appreciated.

Visit us online to learn more:

www.srohousing.org

ABOUT THE BOOK

Anita Nelson, SRO Housing Corporation Chief Executive Officer, is an innovative, energetic and visionary leader with experience in the for-profit and non-profit sectors. Prior to joining SRO Housing Corporation, she was the Director of Operations at the Los Angeles Free Clinic, where she managed a multi-disciplinary team that provided medical, dental, and social services to three sites. She also held the position of Regional Finance Manager at Coca-Cola Bottling Company of Southern California, where she was responsible for providing financial analysis and accounting support to the Southern California region. She received a Bachelor of Science, Finance and Business Economics from the University of Southern California and a Master of Business Administration, Business Management from Pepperdine University. She is responsible for the overall management of SRO Housing Corporation, including all fiscal and administrative management, compliance, and reporting. This book is a result of her belief in the diverse strengths of SRO Housing Corporation's residents and staff.

ABOUT THE AUTHOR

Julia Robinson Shimizu is a writer and non-profit communications specialist whose focus on narrative non-fiction has included stories of homeless, mentally ill, impoverished and formerly incarcerated populations and communities. She received her Associate of Arts in Journalism from Los Angeles Valley College, Bachelor of Arts in Japanese Language and Culture from University of California Los Angeles and Master of Professional Writing from University of Southern California. She interviewed each of the residents and staff featured in this book to craft a collection of stories that appear here and on the SRO Housing Corporation website. www.srohousing.org

ABOUT THE PHOTOGRAPHER

Rachel Murray Framingheddu is a Los Angeles-based Photographer who regularly photographs Red Carpet celebrity events and award ceremonies. She has turned her camera to SRO Housing's Skid Row community with an eye for capturing the beauty and grace of our residents and staff. Some of the portraits are included in this book. www.heartquakepictures.com

Cover design and 30th anniversary logo design by David Ruiz

Made in the USA
San Bernardino, CA
07 February 2015